# THIS TOKEN OF FREEDOM

# THIS TOKEN OF FREEDOM

Jon Helminiak

iUniverse, Inc.
Bloomington

# This Token of Freedom

*Copyright © 2012 by Jon Helminiak.*

*All rights reserved. No part of this book may be used or reproduced by any means, graphic, electronic, or mechanical, including photocopying, recording, taping or by any information storage retrieval system without the written permission of the publisher except in the case of brief quotations embodied in critical articles and reviews.*

*iUniverse books may be ordered through booksellers or by contacting:*

*iUniverse*
*1663 Liberty Drive*
*Bloomington, IN 47403*
*www.iuniverse.com*
*1-800-Authors (1-800-288-4677)*

*Because of the dynamic nature of the Internet, any web addresses or links contained in this book may have changed since publication and may no longer be valid. The views expressed in this work are solely those of the author and do not necessarily reflect the views of the publisher, and the publisher hereby disclaims any responsibility for them.*

*ISBN: 978-1-4759-4370-2 (sc)*
*ISBN: 978-1-4759-4372-6 (hc)*
*ISBN: 978-1-4759-4371-9 (ebk)*

*Library of Congress Control Number: 2012914722*

*Printed in the United States of America*

*iUniverse rev. date: 09/11/2012*

# CONTENTS

Foreword ................................................................... vii
Acknowledgements .................................................. xi
Introduction ............................................................ xiii

I.    Jack Hans Jaffé ................................................... 1
II.   The Islands Shall Not Be Defended:
      Impending War and the Evacuation of Jersey ........ 8
III.  In Brighton and London ..................................... 15
IV.  To America ........................................................ 32
V.   Where in the World Is Wisconsin? ..................... 69
VI.  Back Home to England ...................................... 94
VII. The American Dream ....................................... 119

Afterword ............................................................. 133
About the Author ................................................. 135

# FOREWORD

## *From the Children of Jayne Jaffé Jordan*

We always knew that our mother had a unique childhood. It began on the Isle of Jersey in the English Channel and included five years in America away from her mother during WWII and an eventual immigration to the United States.

Until now, the story was fragmented and had never been put into writing. For our mother's 80th birthday, we decided it was time to document her story so we, our children, and future generations would know about her journey.

This book, inspired by our friend Linda Pontzloff and written by our longtime friend and author Jon Helminiak, is a tribute to our mother. We truly appreciate Jon's countless hours of research and discussions with our mother and other family members in order to complete this book. Jon's knowledge of World War II helped put our mother's story into context, framing it with the global events that surrounded her journey. It's a lesson in history, human emotion, endurance, and love; it is a story that has impacted the lives of many people, friends, and family.

While this is a tribute to our mother, it is also a truly interesting story about an exceptional person. The focus is on "young Jayne Jaffé", but we can assure you that the Jayne we grew up with is a

*Jon Helminiak*

remarkable woman. She is a survivor who is selfless and who raised us with values, beliefs, and an appreciation for life.

This book is for our mother, with love and admiration.

Mike Jordan
Lynne Jordan Schley

*A portion of the proceeds from this book will be donated to the arts in honor of Jayne's love for and involvement in various Milwaukee non-profit organizations.*

*"These cruel, wanton, indiscriminate bombings of London are, of course, a part of Hitler's invasion plans. He hopes, by killing large numbers of civilians, and women and children, that he will terrorize and cow the people of this mighty imperial city . . . Little does he know the spirit of the British nation, or the tough fibre of the Londoners."*
Winston Churchill,
during the London Blitz, Sept. 11, 1940

# ACKNOWLEDGEMENTS

I am grateful to the following people and resources for making this book possible:

**Jayne Jaffé Jordan**, who spent hours answering my questions and recounting, to the best of her ability, her journey from the Isle of Jersey to London and her two trips from London to the United States.

**Mike Jordan** and **Lynne Jordan Schley**, for entrusting me with a family legacy.

**Mary Quinlevan Jordan**, for researching Jayne's transatlantic evacuation crossing.

**Leah Carson**, **Julie Mencel** and **Carolyn Kott Washburne** for their help with manuscript editing.

**Lt. Colonel Raymond Helminiak**, for his editorial suggestions and for his service as a WWII combat pilot as a member of the Eighth Air Force in England. Europe was liberated from Nazi tyranny by men of his caliber who fought and died for freedom.

**Linda Pontzloff**, who suggested that I write this book.

Factual information about the time period was obtained from many resources, but the following books were especially useful:

*Citizens of London*, by Lynne Olson (New York: Random House, 2010)

*Out of Harms Way*, by Jessica Mann (London: Headline Book Publishing, 2005)

Jon Helminiak

# INTRODUCTION

In the summer of 1940, the German Luftwaffe was preparing to destroy Great Britain. The bombing of London began on September 7, 1940 and continued for 56 consecutive days and nights.

To spare their children from witnessing the carnage and from possible death, Londoners evacuated millions of them to safe locations. Their lives would start over in new towns and often with unknown families. Historically, the idea of evacuating an entire generation of children, separating them from their parents, was unprecedented.

This is the story of one of those evacuee children, Jayne Jaffé.

Jayne was born on November 15, 1930. At the time of her birth, the world was at peace, but England was still haunted by memories of World War I, a conflict so ghastly that it was named the "war to end all wars". Yet within the first decade of Jayne's life, preparations were being made for another war, stirred by the fanaticism of Germany's Nazi Party.

World War II forever shaped Jayne's future, as it did the lives of nearly every global citizen. And when Germany declared war on the United Kingdom in 1939, Jayne Jaffé, age nine, began witnessing the best and worst of humanity: war, murder, love, death, separation, tears, euphoria, destruction, and rebuilding.

Although this book is about Jayne, it must also be about her mother, Maureen. Like most children, Jayne's world was shaped by her parents and, in this case, her mother, who made a seemingly unthinkable decision. In advance of the German Blitzkrieg,[1] she decided to send Jayne away during the most formative years of her childhood and entrust her wellbeing to strangers in the United States. Similar decisions were being made by parents throughout England, and many evacuee children and their parents would never be reunited.

Like Jayne, people who lived through the dark years of WWII had their character chiseled into one of resolve and selflessness. Children were raised in an era that demanded self-reliance and perseverance. There were few government programs to provide assistance, so success required hard work, a supportive family, and discipline. It was the only way to survive.

Jayne spent her earliest years on the island of Jersey, one of the four Channel Islands of England that rest in the southern portion of the English Channel. About 45 square miles in size, Jersey lies closer to France than England, and on a clear day the coast of Normandy, France is visible from her eastern shore. Historically, her rocky coast has made it a difficult island to conquer, and many invading wrecks are strewn about her shores.

Jayne and her parents, Maureen and Jack Jaffé, lived in a comfortable stone home in Jersey's rural Pontac Parish. It was close enough to the largest town of St. Helier with its 60,000 people but remote enough to offer peace and privacy. Jack bought the home when he moved to Jersey from London, and before he met Maureen it was essentially a bachelor's residence with an assortment of mismatched furniture, golf trophies, and paintings of no particular value or interest.

But Maureen's feminine touch transformed it into a cozy family abode, decorated with curtains, comfortable furniture, and flowers in window boxes. Scents of homemade breads emanated from the

---

[1.] The literal English translation of "Blitzkrieg" is "lightning war". This military strategy aimed to neutralize the enemy by creating psychological shock and disorganization through intense periods of overwhelming firepower. The Nazis used this tactic to subdue and occupy Belgium, the Netherlands, and Poland.

kitchen as well as the nightly smell of gravy and soups bubbling on the stove.

To Jack, life on the small island was idyllic. The Jersey residents lived in small towns, knew each other well, and could be relied upon to lend a hand. They enjoyed fishing, gardening, lazy summer days, and mild winters. Cows grazed in fields, and men whiled away the evenings in the local pubs. As proprietor of J.H. Jaffé & Company, a distributor of wine and spirits, Jack earned a good living; business was robust, even though he claimed that his friends "drank all the profits".

Jack and Maureen were a popular couple who routinely hosted dinner parties for their friends in their home. In the days before television and radio, entertaining guests was a common way to socialize and relax.

It is in the Jaffé home on a balmy summer evening when Jayne's remarkable story begins.

# - I -

# Jack Hans Jaffé

It was Saturday night on the Isle of Jersey, and Jack Hans Jaffé raised his whiskey glass and addressed his wife and friends.

"Tonight in the Jaffé home, June 8, 1930, let us toast to the Queen and King of England and wish them, by the grace of God, everlasting health, wisdom, and good fortune."

He brought the glass to his lips and paused.

"Oh, I almost forgot." He looked at his young wife Maureen and his guests, then lowered his glass and cleared his throat.

"I'm going to be a father."

The guests roared their approval and advanced toward the expectant couple to congratulate them.

"No, wait!" Jack held up a hand and signaled them to stop.

"There's one last thing." The room fell silent.

"May we toast to peace between Germany and England. A peace that will allow our child, and all of us, to live on Jersey untroubled by the upheavals of warfare." There were murmurs of agreement.

"Now, let us drink."

The men raised and drained their glasses. The women sipped at theirs.

Jack put another handful of coal and wood into the heating stove as the guests helped themselves to slices of roast, potatoes, gravy, and turnip casserole.

"You know what, Jack?" asked George Pooley, one of Jack's business associates. His portly face had become flush with a bit too much whiskey. "You were too young to fight in the first big war, and you're too old to fight now. That is, of course, provided we have to fight the Germans once again."

"For that I have my mother and father to thank, don't I? They timed me quite well." Jack brushed his hands clean of soot and poured himself another whiskey. "And even if we do have a war, being a father at my age won't be so bad, either. I'll focus on raising my child instead of raising a bloody rifle above the mud wall of a battlefield trench."

Maureen added, "I don't think Germany would dare to fight the Crown again."

The conversations continued about war, children, Jersey, and England until the wee hours of the morning. Guests were always reluctant to leave; the Jaffé home was a comfortable retreat, and Jack and Maureen were engaging hosts. Best of all, there was always ample whiskey and wine, provided by Jack's business, J.H. Jaffé & Company.

Unlike Maureen, Jack Hans Jaffé had been previously married and had an adult daughter. Born in London in 1883, he developed into a handsome, athletic, and charismatic man. His well-proportioned, stocky frame was usually dressed in fine suits or sport jackets. His grin and easy laugh put others at ease, and his firm handshake punctuated his honest reputation.

By 1910, he was recognized as one of London's best golfers, playing in tournaments hosted by prestigious golf clubs throughout England. He was also a champion "punter" who raced in a punt boat, a wooden, flat-bottomed vessel with a square-cut bow. The punt, about the size of a small rowboat, was propelled by pushing a long pole off the river bottom. Weekend punters' races on London's Thames River were popular among participants and spectators alike, and Jack was one of the best at his craft.

Jack's good looks and athletic skills made him popular among the ladies, but he had little time for courtship. Then one evening, while he dined with friends at a London pub, one of his pals claimed he knew a "cheeky single girl". Would Jack like to meet her? The friend offered to arrange an introduction at the cinema on Victoria Street, where she worked as the movie house manager.

Jack accepted, knowing that he had little to lose. He could attend the silent feature film (all movies in the early 1900s were without sound) and meet the girl named Maud. They'd enjoy the movie together, and if they were attracted to each other, it would be a bonus.

On the evening they met, both Jack and Maud were equally smitten. They courted for several months, and eventually Jack asked Maud for her hand in marriage. It was 1906, and he was 23 years old.

Within the year, Maud gave birth to a girl whom she and Jack named Joy. Her friends and family nicknamed the girl "Pix", and Jack, Maud, and Pix lived happily together for about 20 years.

But then, for unknown reasons, Jack and Maud divorced. Given the stigma placed on divorce in the 1920s, especially between Catholic couples, their reasons for parting must have been considerable. Furthermore, Jack and Maud were considered upstanding, honest, and committed to each other.

By the time they divorced, Pix had grown into a stunning woman in her early twenties. She had honed her natural musical talents into a career, playing piano and singing at local theaters and private events. With Pix living her own adult life, Jack decided to move to the Isle of Jersey. It was time to start over, and Jersey would be a tranquil place to begin.

Within days after arriving on Jersey, Jack joined the LaMoye and Royal Jersey Golf Clubs. Soon he was appointed captain of the LaMoye golf team and won many club championships.

Being active in the golf clubs was an efficient way for Jack to expand his business and social networks, including the circle of single Jersey females. Already he was enamored with a girl named Maureen Conway who worked at the LaMoye Golf Club. She was 23 years his junior, but undeterred by the age gap, he made his romantic intentions known, and Maureen was receptive.

Initially they chatted casually at the club or ate together when Maureen was off work and Jack had finished his rounds of golf. But the club lacked privacy, and Jack and Maureen grew weary of the disapproving stares of their club friends and work colleagues. Many felt it was inappropriate for an older man to date such a young, innocent girl.

So they took their courtship elsewhere: to pubs, beaches, and parks. And despite their generational differences, they developed an easy rapport. Maureen liked Jack's easygoing style. This athletic, savvy businessman always knew how to have fun between responsibilities. Jack loved a strong drink, a good party, and close friends.

In turn, Jack thought Maureen very mature for her age. She had a strong constitution, seemed very determined, was quick to laugh, and enjoyed being social. Like Jack, she was of strong and stout build, yet at 5 feet 3 inches tall, she appeared very feminine. Her straight, auburn hair fell to her shoulders, and she carried herself with poise and distinction.

In short, Jack and Maureen worked well together as a couple.

On September 5, 1929, Jack and Maureen were married in St. Helier, and Maureen moved into Jack's home outside of town. There they began their life together, filled with the promise of longevity, love, family, friends, and stability.

Yet to the east, the resurrected sabers of the German army were rattling. But neither Jack nor Maureen gave it much thought. Their life on the little island was as safe and secure as it could be. Maureen had a successful and loving husband, a warm home, and good friends. Both she and Jack looked forward to living happily ever after.

\* \* \*

On the days before Maureen was expected to give birth, the Jaffé kitchen was prepared with supplies needed for home birthing: bowls, antiseptic, towels, and blankets. There were only a few small clinics on Jersey, and its doctors and beds were reserved for seriously ill patients. Most children were delivered at home by parents, family doctors, or midwives.

On the morning of November 15, 1930, Maureen Jaffé awoke and told Jack it was time. Jack lit a candle, took Maureen's hand, and led her down the stairs into the kitchen. There he helped her lie on the blanket-covered kitchen table, and he summoned the family doctor who lived nearby. By midmorning, Jack held a crying baby girl.

Jayne Jaffé was born.

The Jaffés adjusted well to their new daughter. Jack continued to work at J.H. Jaffé & Company while Maureen tended to Jayne and looked after the household. It was a relationship typical of the times: father earned the income, and mother raised the children.

Compared to other families on the island, the Jaffés lived well. Most others on Jersey weren't so fortunate; they lived in tiny flats or small houses, subsisting on meager incomes from menial labor and farming.

But the Jaffés frequently hosted parties and attended functions at the LaMoye and Royal Jersey Golf Clubs. Jayne was enrolled in a private school, the Jersey Girls College, in nearby St. Helier. During the summer, the Jaffés sailed across the English Channel to visit relatives in London, a trip that very few people could afford at the time.

Jersey provided Jayne with a fine country childhood. She grew up between the countryside and the sea, romping in the fields and building sandcastles on the beach. There were farms with sheep and cows and fishing boats whose crews' unloaded fresh fish in the harbors. From the top of the hills, she could spread her arms in the crisp sea winds and pretend she was flying like one of those new machines called airplanes. In downtown St. Helier, the main promenade was always filled with men and women in their best clothing, the women holding umbrellas to shield themselves from the sun, and the men in knickers, ties, and hats.

Without a brother or sister, Jayne was included in most of the adult activities, and she adjusted well to the older crowd. She enjoyed school and befriended many children her own age. Her plucky and independent spirit enabled her to adapt easily to nearly every situation, and both young and old found her to be pleasant company.

As for Jack, he was proud of Jayne and enjoyed his second round of fatherhood at age 47. He would often invite Pix, his daughter from his first marriage, to visit Jersey and stay with the new Jaffé family, which she often did, along with her husband Con Boddington. Con was a career military man, and his strong physique and chiseled face complemented Pix's movie-star looks. They made a stunning couple, and by all accounts they got along well with Maureen and Jayne. For the rest of his life, Con affectionately referred to himself as Jayne's "big brother".

Jayne's Jersey childhood was untroubled – with one exception. Although she had a warm home, loving parents, and friends of all ages, she worried about her father, who seemed weary and less chipper and was plagued by a nagging cough. While her mother claimed otherwise, Jayne suspected something was wrong. She would ask her father how he felt, and he'd reply with a smile, "I'm fit and happy!" Then he would sigh and add, "Your Daddy is just a little tired, that's all." Maureen did what she could for her husband, taking him to the family doctor and ensuring his comfort at home.

But on April 27, 1939, the championship golfer and businessman, charismatic and handsome Jack Hans Jaffé, suddenly died. He was 57 years old. The official cause of death was lung abscess, a bacterial caused form of pneumonia.[2]

Maureen, who was emotionally shaken by the passing of her husband, now faced the challenge of single parenthood. But there were other, more alarming issues that could affect not only the future of Maureen and Jayne but every citizen of the Channel Islands.

---

[2.] Before antibiotics, lung abscess was a devastating disease. One-third of sufferers died, another one-third recovered, and the remainder developed debilitating illnesses such as recurrent abscesses, chronic emphysema, or bronchitis. Although surgery was often considered a treatment option in the past, its role has greatly diminished because today's patients respond to prolonged antibiotic therapy.

Just 400 miles to the east in Germany, Adolph Hitler was making headlines. The *London Telegraph*, England's most widely-read newspaper, printed unsettling reports of a rapidly expanding German military with sophisticated warships, tanks, and aircraft.

Already in 1938, German troops had invaded Austria. The country succumbed without resistance, and its people were now living under Nazi oppression. By March 1939, all of Czechoslovakia[3] was under German control, breaking the terms of the Munich Agreement that Hitler had accepted.[4] Despite calls for help from Czechoslovakia's government, neither Britain nor France was prepared to intervene, naively hoping that Hitler would end his conquests with Czechoslovakia's capitulation.

There was concern in Parliament, however, that Poland might be Hitler's next target. Many lawmakers believed that the bombastic Hitler was plotting to occupy all of Europe, including England. Should he act on his ambitions, it was likely that the Channel Islands, being the closest English territory to Germany, would be the first British soil invaded.

And so, silently and reluctantly, the residents of Jersey began contemplating what they would do in the event of the unthinkable: an assault on their island home by the German armed forces.

---

[3.] Czechoslovakia now consists of the independent nations of the Czech Republic and Slovakia.

[4.] The Munich Agreement, signed in September 1938 by the leaders of Germany, Britain, France, and Italy, agreed that the former German territory of the Sudetenland in Czechoslovakia would be returned to Germany in exchange for Hitler's promise that he would make no additional territorial claims. British Prime Minister Neville Chamberlain met with Hitler three times in September 1938 in an attempt to convince him to sign the pact, which he ultimately did. Chamberlain returned to England as the triumphant hero; newspaper photographs showed him holding the treaty that declared "Peace In Our Time". Months later, it was clear that Chamberlain and the other leaders had been duped. Hitler's ambitions of conquest were far-ranging and included the United Kingdom.

## - II -

## The Islands Shall Not Be Defended: Impending War and the Evacuation of Jersey

In 1939, the English people were in no mood for another war, and the nation was not prepared to fight one.

Memories of World War I, just 20 years earlier, haunted nearly every British adult. World War I had been so horrific that it was referred to as the "Great War". More than 800,000 British men, or 20 percent of the male population, died in battles fought in trenches, in cavalry-style advances, and in fogs of poison gas. The dead left behind grieving parents, girlfriends, widows, children, and friends. For these people – nearly everybody over age 30 – the thought of another war was inconceivable.

Prime Minister Neville Chamberlain and much of the British Parliament agreed. The prevailing sentiment was that the military should not have priority for government funding. As a result, the armed forces of Great Britain were gradually depleted and the military dwindled to its lowest number of soldiers in decades. The British naval fleet consisted of ponderous and under-armed WWI-era steamships, and the British Air Force was virtually nonexistent, with just several squadrons of outdated fighters and no heavy bombers. Pilots were young, and few were combat-ready.

Conversely, since 1934, Germany had pursued an aggressive military buildup to avenge what it viewed as a humiliating defeat in WWI. The newly-elected Nazi Party set about rebuilding its military with sophisticated aircraft, battleships, submarines, tanks, and artillery.

The Nazi Party also fueled a rebound of radical German pride. Newsreels showed thousands of goose-stepping, swastika-clad soldiers parading down the avenues of Berlin, hailed by thousands of waving citizens. Hitler himself was a charismatic figure, assuring the German people through fiery speeches accompanied by wild gesticulation that their years of economic depression were over. Germany was to be great once again.

But as with all dictators, "greatness" for Hitler meant persecution of citizens who held beliefs deemed incompatible with the state. It also meant the occupation of other nations, government control of the news media, conscription of large industries, and nationalized health care. Certain religions, especially Judaism, were deemed incompatible with Nazi Party goals. Slowly and incrementally, the German population was weaned from self-reliance to government dependency. With promises of the "good life" ahead, the German citizenry embraced the Nazi Party without recognizing the toll it would take on their nation.

British Prime Minister Chamberlain calculated that Hitler's imperialistic ambitions would end with the occupation of the Sudetenland in 1938. He even traveled to Germany to meet with the leader of the Reich and found the Führer to be cordial and engaging. Hitler accommodated Chamberlain in luxurious chalets and bestowed upon him the finest German hospitality of ample food and beverage. He told Chamberlain that he had no designs on England; he even liked England! So, despite Hitler's track record of deceitful negotiations with other nations, Chamberlain naively assured his people that their island nation would be safe.

Many disagreed. Winston Churchill, a veteran of WWI and long-standing Member of Parliament, warned that Hitler's ambitions would extend across Europe and beyond. Taking advantage of his pulpit as an elder British statesman, Churchill used parliamentary speeches, newspaper articles, and meetings with foreign dignitaries to spread his conviction that a storm of military aggression was brewing in Germany.

Churchill claimed that the facts, and the conclusions to be drawn from them, were clear. Intelligence reports confirmed massive military buildups. In addition, Hitler's ambitions for European domination, despite his charm and words to the contrary, were well documented. England could not afford to ignore them.

Churchill further accused Prime Minister Chamberlain of gambling with Britain's sovereignty by championing policies that appeased Hitler instead of standing up to his aggressions. It was highly probable, Churchill argued, that Hitler's conquests could eventually include the lightly armed British homeland.

Then, at 4:45 a.m. on September 1, 1939, 1.5 million Nazi soldiers invaded Poland. This occupation was different from the takeovers of Austria and Czechoslovakia. The Poles resisted, so the Nazis retaliated by massacring innocent civilians, including children. Newspaper and radio accounts described German fighter aircraft strafing children, tanks destroying historic buildings, and Jews being shot or imprisoned. A photo of a young girl grieving over the bullet-riddled body of her sister in a Polish field brought global attention to the savagery of the Nazi regime.

As a senior and respected Member of Parliament, Winston Churchill responded to the occupation of Poland by addressing the British people:

> We must not underrate the gravity of the task before us . . . This is not a question of fighting for Danzig or fighting for Poland. We are fighting to save the whole world from the pestilence of Nazi tyranny . . .

Increasingly, the British people began to agree that Churchill, the long-winded orator and prolific writer, was right. And so did the majority of Parliament. On May 10, 1940, Prime Minister Neville Chamberlain resigned, and Winston Churchill was appointed to replace him.

Inspired by Churchill's leadership, the British people began preparing themselves for their second war with Germany in two decades.

\* \* \*

Maureen and the other people of Jersey nervously read newspaper reports and listened to scratchy radio transmissions about the Nazis' rapid military conquests.

Since the Channel Islands were the closest British territory to Germany, they were in a vulnerable position for occupation. Already Jersey residents had seen squadrons of German bombers flying overhead. Intelligence reports in 1939 confirmed that a German assault force of two battalions was preparing to invade nearby Guernsey Island, where nearly 50 islanders had already been killed during a German aerial bombardment of its harbor.

Just as troubling as the civilian deaths on Guernsey was the lack of response by the British military. No British troops or warships were sent to defend the islands, and rumors circulated that none would be forthcoming. Yet historically England had always come to the aid of her possessions and territories. Surely, thought Maureen and the other residents of Jersey, the Channel Islands would be sufficiently armed to repel the imperialistic Germans.

But on June 15, 1940, the British government and Winston Churchill reluctantly agreed that the Channel Islands were of no strategic importance and would not be defended. Jersey residents resented Churchill's decision. Were the islands, the oldest possession of the Crown, of so little importance to Britain that Parliament would willingly allow them to fall?

Although the thought of German occupation was repugnant, it was strategically the correct decision. The Channel Islands would be of little value to the Germans, other than the propaganda value of having occupied British territory. And the British military would be better used defending London, which was likely to be the target of a German aerial bombardment.

Ultimately, Churchill did not abandon the welfare of the island people. He consulted with the islands' elected government officials to formulate a plan for citizen evacuation, insisting that the government needed to make this gesture. Parliament could not allow British citizens to become German subjects against their will. As a result, England would make available as many ships as possible to evacuate certain segments of the island citizens, primarily women and children. The only men who could leave via government ships were those who had elected to join the military.

The remaining population of the islands would have to endure German occupation.

Faced with the death of her husband and the uncertain future of Jersey, Maureen decided that there was little incentive to remain on the island. Further, the business of J.H. Jaffé & Company was now in the good hands of Jack's former business associate, George Pooley, and his wife Nora. Maureen retained a percentage of the business, and the Pooleys reliably gave Maureen her share of the earnings.

With probable German occupation, evacuation made sense. It was time for Maureen and Jayne to start new lives. The most convenient place to relocate was to England proper. Passenger ferries regularly plied the 8-hour, 118-mile crossing of the English Channel, arriving in Southhampton. But with occupation looming, those boats were fully booked and thousands of people were on the waiting lists. The docks were crowded with women, children, and the elderly, who hoped for standing room on any vessel that might allow them to board without a reservation.

However, with government ships and some private vessels available for evacuation, securing passage would be less daunting. Maureen finalized her decision to leave, and then she had to tell Jayne.

When she heard of her mother's plans, Jayne seemed untroubled by the idea of moving, and she may even have been enthused. London was one of those places you read about in school and heard about on the radio but seldom visited. And although Jayne had traveled there with her mother and father years ago, it was still a magical destination for a young girl living on little Jersey Island. It would be a new adventure, and as long as her mother was with her, she knew she'd be safe.

With Jayne accepting what lay ahead, Maureen posted a letter to her sister, Cynthia Agnes Conway Johnson (nicknamed "Adj"), who was living in the coastal town of Brighton for the summer. In her letter, Maureen inquired whether she and Jayne might come and live with Adj, at least until the Nazi threat of Channel Island occupation had passed.

Adj replied that they would be welcome. She also warned that Brighton, and all of England, was preparing for war. Certain foods were already in short supply, and petrol (gasoline) was being rationed. Since Brighton was along the English Channel, it was on the front lines of Nazi bombers flying north from Germany. Batteries of anti-aircraft guns were being stationed along the shoreline, but they could not destroy every German bomber or fighter. Air attack, fire, destruction, and death were still possible.

Maureen did not tell Jayne about Adj's warnings, preferring to keep an upbeat demeanor about their impending move. Even if Adj's words did come true, enduring German bombs would be preferable to living under Nazi occupation of Jersey.

Of greater concern to Maureen was being able to financially support themselves. Aunt Adj was relatively well off, but Maureen did not want to depend upon her financial blessings. So, for extra money, Maureen sold many unwanted household items. Then she packed only personal necessities into two large trunks that would accompany them on the voyage. She placed their remaining possessions into large crates that were taken to a warehouse for storage. There was no guarantee the stored items would be safe; invading Nazis were known to confiscate anything of value and ship it to Germany.

As for the Jaffé home, Maureen decided to rent it, and the Pooleys agreed to be the landlords in her absence. Many Jersey families who remained behind would welcome living in the elegant Jaffé residence. It would also be an attractive place for invading

German officers to reside, a repugnant thought that Maureen did not want to contemplate.

In early June 1940, after packing their personal items, Maureen and Jayne went about the somber task of bidding their friends farewell. The goodbyes were brief and stoic. The mood was one of fear more than sorrow, and only brief tears were shed. Keeping a "stiff upper lip" was the British way, no matter how dire the circumstances. Jayne and Maureen were doing what they had to do. It was, in effect, a business decision for the well-being of the Jaffé family.

Moreover, parting was symbolic of the fact that the lives of everyone on Jersey were about to change dramatically. Those staying behind realized that they might be living under German occupation or even be deported to Germany. Those leaving were taking a journey into the unknown, often to cities and towns far removed from the tranquility and comforts of Jersey.

A friend gave Maureen and Jayne a ride to the dock, which was crowded with passengers waiting to board. After checking their trunks at the freight station (passengers were allowed only one trunk each), Maureen took Jayne's hand, and they slowly made their way to the boarding ramp.

The ship did not look like it was built for people, and it wasn't. Many government evacuation vessels were freighters, conscripted from private companies whose business was transporting coal, ore, grain, and industrial supplies. Onboard, Maureen found their boat to be filthy, with limited seating and only a few bathrooms to accommodate the hundreds of passengers. Since the ship's decks were packed to standing room, some evacuees crawled into the lifeboats that hung over the ocean, suspended by metal braces.

As the freighter got underway, Maureen and Jayne stood on the stern of the ship and watched Jersey disappear. When it was out of sight, Maureen and Jayne pushed their way through the passengers toward the bow. "Brighton is out there," Maureen said, pointing north. Jayne nodded.

From that point on, Maureen never looked back at Jersey. Their life was ahead of them, and that is where her thoughts needed to be.

## - III -

## *In Brighton and London*

Throughout the course of history, tens of thousands of ships have arrived and departed from the port of Southampton. From its harbor have left wooden ships sailing on voyages of discovery across the Atlantic, merchant vessels heading to Africa and Persia for commerce, and, during WWII, American and British vessels headed for the shores of France to begin the liberation of Europe.

Now, in June 1940, Maureen and Jayne stood shoulder to shoulder on the deck of their ship, scanning the crowds at the Southampton dock. Maureen hoped she would recognize Adj, for it had been many years since they had last seen each other. Jayne wondered if all her mother's stories about her "fun auntie" were true. She desperately hoped Adj would like her and that they would all get along.

The ship's horn blew twice, and the gangplanks were lowered to the concrete pier, where dock men in blue jumpsuits worked to secure them. It was always exciting when a ship came to port: the crews scurrying about and crowds on both ship and land frantically waving, hoping to catch a glimpse of their friends or loved ones.

As Maureen and Jayne descended the gangplank, Jayne felt her mother's hand grab her shoulder. "There's Adj! That's her!" Jayne saw a tall woman in a long dress and flowery hat waving vigorously in the distance. Jayne said, "That's Aunt Adj?" She looked so different, as if by her dress and manner she purposely tried to stand out from everybody else.

Maureen assured her that it was indeed Aunt Adj, and furthermore "We're damn lucky she's here." Jayne rarely heard her mother swear, so she knew that their successful rendezvous with Adj was a relief to her and a secure beginning to their new life.

On the train trip from Southampton to Brighton, Adj and Maureen became reacquainted. There was much news to share: the passing of Jack, England's preparations for war, and the status of the people who remained behind on Jersey. There were also updates about friends and relatives. Absent from the conversation was any discussion about what Maureen and Jayne intended to do with their lives now that they had left Jersey. Perhaps they assumed, like many did, that the war would end quickly or that Hitler would back down. In that case, Maureen and Jayne would return home within the year.

Aunt Adj was indeed an interesting lady. Far different from most British women, she was vivacious and confident. She sang opera, loved to travel, and owned a flat in London and a country house in Brighton. She was thoroughly enjoying her life as a single female. Later in life, she traveled the world as a passenger on cargo ships, taking months to reach exotic destinations and afterward raving about the wonderful onboard service.

Adj had not always been so carefree; she had been married twice and lost both husbands, one in the First World War and the second to natural causes. With her first husband, she had a daughter, Mary, who was now in her early twenties and living on her own in London.

Aunt Adj's seemingly rebellious and independent spirit was attractive to Jayne, and she found herself reassured by Adj's positive energy. If Adj had survived the loss of two husbands, traveled the world alone, and managed her own affairs, she could surely look after the well-being of her two new house guests, even during a war.

Compared to sleepy Jersey, Brighton seemed a cosmopolitan town of grandeur. Its magnificent sights included the Royal Pavilion, built in the early nineteenth century as the home for the Prince Regent. This long white building featured Indian-style architecture with onion-shaped domes and a posh oriental interior. Two imposing piers at the wide beach housed restaurants, arcade halls, and pubs. Then there was the Grand Hotel, built in 1864, where notables and the wealthy stayed while in town.

Jayne thought Brighton seemed a fun place to live, and it was. Being on the sea, and just over an hour by train from London, it was one of Britain's popular vacation towns. It offered entertainment, wide beaches, nightlife, and music to suit nearly every holiday palate. Brighton proved to be a comfortable transition town, and Maureen and Jayne smoothly eased into it.

With all of Brighton's diversions, their thoughts of Jersey were diminishing. The town possessed a holiday atmosphere, and people drank, ate, and enjoyed themselves, perhaps to forget about the impending war. The weather was warm and sunny, and life was marvelous.

Sundays were especially fun, when Adj served a juicy beef roast and a sugary homemade pie. At night, they listened to entertaining radio dramas that used dialogue, music, and sound effects to help the listener imagine the characters and story. The dramas were performed live in the radio studios, and many of the actors were as popular as the cinema stars of the day.

On Sunday evening, June 30, 1940, the radio drama was interrupted by a British Broadcasting Corporation newsman with an urgent bulletin: "This evening, we have official word that the Island of Guernsey, one of the Channel Islands, has been occupied by German forces. There was no opposition from the island population." The newsman continued providing sketchy details and then concluded: "We now return you to your regular broadcast."

Adj turned off the radio. They sat silently, Maureen with her head bowed, Adj staring out the window, and Jayne looking at both of them, wondering what it all meant. Maureen said softly, "My friends, those people, what will become of them all?"

Jayne finally asked, "Will the Germans go to Jersey next?" Maureen cleared her throat and nodded. "Yes, I'm sure they will."

Adj rose, went into the kitchen, and returned with a candle. She placed it on the table near the radio, lit the wick, and said, "We must say a prayer." Maureen spoke a few words about safety, strength, protection, England, family, and faith. Everyone said "Amen."

Although Maureen was Catholic, she and Jayne seldom attended church. Yet on this night, she needed to draw upon God's protection and goodness, for it was beyond the ability of any mortal being to look after her people on Jersey. She wondered what the Nazis would do to her home, the Pooleys, her friends, and the belongings she had left behind. And although she was safe in Brighton, she still felt personally violated by the invading Germans. In a way, she was relieved that Jack wasn't there to witness it all.

Life went on, albeit subdued, for Maureen and Jayne in Brighton. A pall of fear hung in the air, for now that the Germans had taken British soil, their next stop might likely be the British southern coast, maybe Brighton itself. So by late July, Adj announced it was time to leave for London.

The potential of a German invasion notwithstanding, the Brighton cottage provided only temporary respite from Adj's life in London. After a month or two, she usually developed the urge to return to the big city, where she had a robust social life and minor business to attend to. She was never sure how long she would be there, but it would probably be just long enough to fill her love of urban excitement before she began missing the peace and quiet of Brighton.

Since Jayne was comfortable in Brighton, Maureen considered asking Adj if she and Jayne could remain behind for just another week. But Maureen also needed to find work, and London would be better suited for a successful job search. So in early August, everyone packed their belongings and boarded the train for the hour-long ride to London. As they watched the green countryside pass outside the window, Adj reassured them that London would be the best place to ride out the war. There were ample bomb shelters, better hospitals and assistance centers, and a greater supply of goods, food, and supplies.

There was also Aunt Grace, the sister of Adj and Maureen. "And who wouldn't want to be around Aunt Grace?" Adj asked rhetorically.

There was truth to that, thought Maureen. Grace Conway always seemed to be where there was an important party, often attended by celebrities. Even Jayne remembered Aunt Grace as somebody who was somewhat famous. And within the expanding world of movies and movie theaters, she was.

As movie editor for the *London Catholic Herald*, Aunt Grace was one of London's most recognized socialites. She was on the exclusive invitation list for the premier showing of major motion pictures in London, each of which was followed a grand party attended by the film's actors and actresses.

Adj said that if they were lucky, Aunt Grace might ask all of them to attend the premier showing of a new movie that was already a hit in America. "I think it's called *Gone with the Wind*, or something like that," she said.

As the train neared Waterloo Station in central London, Jayne was taken with the numbers of cars and people. They seemed to be everywhere, with the automobiles honking, bicyclists weaving between traffic, and sidewalks crowded with pedestrians. It was all a bit frightening and not anything like Brighton.

Adj hailed a taxi for the short ride to her flat. Adj's flat was modest, with a kitchen, small living area, and two bedrooms. Maureen and Adj took turns cooking breakfast and dinner. Lunch was usually just a snack or a light sandwich.

Throughout London, preparations were being made for war. Posters in stores and in the subway stations urged citizens to "keep calm and carry on." (This saying would eventually become the nation's rallying cry during the London Blitzkrieg.) Rationing cards had been issued for some foods, including butter, sugar, tea, cheese, bacon, and meat. Often, Adj or Maureen waited in line for these commodities, only to discover that the store was sold out when they reached the front.

Most alarming to Jayne were the large posters seen in stores and subway stations that implored parents to move their children out of London. One poster read: "Mothers, send them out of London. Give them a chance of great safety and health." Beneath those words was a photograph of a young brother and sister, the brother's hands on the girl's shoulders as if to comfort and protect her. Both looked worried. Another poster showed a fatherly man bent over at the waist and shaking his finger at a young boy. The caption read: "Leave this to us, Sonny. You'd ought to be out of London!"

Jayne asked her mother about the posters. Maureen said that, yes, because of the possibility of German bombs, many children might have to leave London for their safety. But then she added that she wasn't sure if Jayne would have to move again. They had just arrived in London, and it was too soon to know.

Jayne had assumed London was her final stop. But if it was going to be bombed, would she have to pack up and go somewhere else? Jayne noticed her mother never said "we" might have to move, so Jayne wondered if she might have to leave by herself. She decided not to worry about it; there was enough to see and do in London, with all of its newness. London was appealing to this young girl, with discoveries to be made daily.

Some of the discoveries were frightening. Loud sirens, for example, would wail daily. They were not the sirens Jayne was used to hearing on police cars or ambulances but whining, piercing sirens that emanated from the tops of buildings. When this happened, people on the streets dashed to stairs and disappeared underground.

Adj explained that the sirens meant German bombers had been sighted and soon there would be bombs falling on London or on cities to the north, such as Manchester or Liverpool. Buildings would be destroyed, and many people killed. The only safe place was underground, in the subway stations or designated bomb shelters.

By midsummer 1940, the citizens of London became accustomed to bombing raids and to taking shelter several times a day or night. Most of the alarms were triggered by the sighting of German aircraft formations along the coast, flying north. Many of these aircraft were only performing reconnaissance, gathering information and photographs for German military command. But still, a few bombs would be dropped indiscriminately, leveling buildings and sometimes even killing people who elected not to seek underground safety.

The shelters were crammed with people whose combined body heat made the environment uncomfortably hot and stuffy. If hours passed before the "all clear" siren sounded, many relieved themselves on the subway tracks, which added a repulsive stench to the air. Jayne was happy when she could re-emerge into fresh air on the streets, where she sometimes saw other children scrambling for souvenirs among the shell casings and shrapnel from nearby bomb explosions.

Despite the repeated air raids and the escalating war, Londoners went about their business with their typical plucky and happy spirits. Pubs were crowded at lunch, the markets bustled, and business went on as usual. But there was a pall in the air, something artificial about daily life. Londoners would smile and laugh and "keep calm and carry on", as the poster implored them to do. Maureen sensed that most people were worried and frightened, but a good Briton would never let on about that. It was important to keep spirited and happy, even in the face of war. It was the British way.

After a week, Jayne had begun to feel more at home in London, but it still seemed big, foreign, and impersonal. In Jersey, she awoke to the sounds of wind, hoof beats, and birds and to the scent of breakfast cooking in the kitchen. In London, the sounds were harsh and abrasive and not at all soothing: sirens, honking cars, voices of people on the streets, and vendors shouting about wares for sale on their carts.

But Jayne had other worrisome things on her mind. Her mother had not enrolled her in school, and many of their belongings remained in the trunks, still packed. That, along with the posters asking parents to relocate their children out of the city, convinced Jayne that they might move once again.

Jayne did not know to where, nor did she much care, as long as her mother went with her. But as she was about to discover, Maureen had already made quiet arrangements for a move to a place much farther away than the English countryside.

\* \* \*

By late August 1939, about one year before Jayne, Maureen, and Adj arrived in London, the British government issued orders that certain citizens be evacuated from cities that were considered to be in danger of German bombs, including London, Coventry, Birmingham, and Portsmouth. These "certain" citizens included schoolchildren and their teachers, mothers with children younger than five years old, pregnant women, and some disabled people.

The idea of evacuating an entire generation of children, separating them from their mothers and fathers, was historically unprecedented. History is replete with stories of families fleeing aggression, but never had children been sent away on their own. Many Britons found the idea unthinkable. One parent wrote that sending children away was a "monstrous thing to do; even the despised Nazis think that no children under 10 should be evacuated without their parents."

A columnist for *The Lady* argued:

> It should be said that children should not be regarded as charming pets to be kept away from real life. They, too, are British people, and they might be better British people because of their patriotism being tested in their early years. There is no way of saving children entirely from the dangers of modern war.

Others, particularly veterans of World War I, countered that the children needed to be spared the nightmarish memories of warfare. "I didn't spend four years in the trenches to have my children go through a war," said one vet. Another veteran of that war, the historian H.G. Clark, wrote that he had witnessed what happens when one country overruns another, including "lost children wandering around all alone, disemboweled babies on roadsides, seeing parents and relatives die in front of you".

Both pro and con arguments like these were exchanged throughout the summer of 1940, and mothers, fathers, and grandparents often disagreed on whether or not to evacuate their children and grandchildren. Some families became divided over the final decision, resulting in rifts that lasted until well after the war's conclusion.

Ultimately, most parents, like Maureen, decided that it was in the best interests of their children's future to move them out of the city. Not only would they be spared injury or death, but they also would escape potential German occupation and the loss of their personal freedom.

To coordinate the evacuations, Parliament established the Children's Overseas Reception Board (CORB). The enormity of the board's task was daunting as more than three million people met the criteria for evacuation. Some families were fortunate to have relatives living in Scotland, Ireland, or the English countryside. For those parents, shipping their children away was less difficult, both logistically and emotionally.

But for most children, not only did transportation from the cities have to be arranged, but suitable accommodations had to be found in regions deemed safe, primarily in the countryside, where thousands of rural families agreed to accept the refugees.

On the day the evacuation orders were issued, August 31, 1939, children were sent to school with their luggage, and by afternoon they were taken to railroad stations where they would board the trains taking them to unknown destinations to live with unknown people. As they waited to embark, adults tied a label onto their blazers noting their name and the name of their school. Each child was given a square box containing a gas mask as well as a small canvas satchel containing rations that included a tin of sardines, a packet of currants, and a tin of luncheon meat.

Parents were forbidden to accompany their children to the railroad stations, but many wailing and weeping mothers, who had reconsidered their decision to send their children away, broke through police barricades at the schools to retrieve them. Within three days, nearly 1.5 million children were transported out of London and resettled in the countryside under Operation Pied Piper.

Days later, parents received postcards telling them where their children were located and with whom they were living. The notice offered only marginal comfort. Parents became overwrought, knowing the host families might instill their children with different value systems, foods, routines, and schooling. And mothers and fathers who remained behind also worried: "*Will I survive the inevitable German bombs?*"

Over time, it became evident that there were not enough families in the "safe" zones of England to accommodate all of the children whose parents wanted them evacuated. To help, the British Commonwealth nations, including South Africa, New Zealand, Australia, and Canada, opened their ports. Each country created a government bureau to coordinate relocation on their soil and cooperated with Britain's CORB.

Although the British Commonwealth nations were satisfactory relocation alternatives, the most desirable country for evacuation was the United States of America. Not only was America much closer by ship, but it was the "promised land": the nation with the most wealth, the most integrity, and the best standards of living. America was a dream destination for many Europeans who sought opportunities to better their standards of living and liberate themselves from nations where hopes of advancement were tethered by the shackles of strict class structures. Maureen knew many families who saved shilling after shilling until there was enough to send a daughter or son to America for a better life.

But by 1940, America had adopted strict immigration laws, so CORB did not endorse or coordinate evacuations to the United States. Therefore, these evacuations needed to be private undertakings, making them more complex to arrange.

At first, Maureen considered sending Jayne to Toronto, where "friends of a friend" lived and had agreed to welcome Jayne. But at some point, and nobody knows precisely when, Maureen determined that the safest and most promising place for Jayne to live was the United States, even though she only had distant relatives and no friends living there.

It didn't matter; a 1940 Gallup poll indicated that five million American families were willing to welcome children from Britain into their homes. American newspapers urged: "Mothers of England, from across the sea, from the cities and mountains and prairies of the west, your children are safe and happy in our wide land. Send us more of them."

To prepare for the potential influx of refugee children, the United States government established the U.S. Committee for the Care of European Children, with Eleanor Roosevelt as its honorary president and Marshall Field III as chairman. More than 170 branches were organized across the nation, and families that desired to host evacuees were required to register and undergo extensive interviews with their local branch representatives.

With the organizational structures in place, Maureen went about arranging for Jayne's evacuation to America. There were formal matters to satisfy, including obtaining a passport, filing paperwork with British authorities, and finding an American organization to sponsor Jayne's arrival and coordinate her eventual settlement. If Jayne were evacuating to a Commonwealth nation, which America was not, many of these matters would have been handled by CORB.

Knowing the logistical and financial challenges faced by parents who wanted their children sent to America, many businesses offered to help. One of those was the *Boston Evening Transcript* newspaper which, along with its readers, funded and coordinated the relocation of 500 British children to the U.S. via Boston. Jayne was selected to be one of the fortunate 500.

The packing of personal items was regulated by CORB, and even though Jayne was not sailing under their auspices, Maureen thought it wise to comply. CORB recommended that, in addition to their passport, papers, and identity cards, girls being evacuated should take only the following personal items:

    Vest
    Pair of knickers
    Petticoat
    2 pairs of stockings
    6 handkerchiefs
    Slip

Blouse
Cardigan
2 skirts
2 dresses
Comb
Overcoat or mackintosh
Towel
Soap
Face cloth
Toothbrush and brushing powder
Boots or shoes
Plimsolls [athletic shoes]
Sandwiches
Packet of nuts and raisins
Dry biscuits
Barley sugar
Apple

Maureen also gave Jayne 10 British pounds of spending money, the equivalent of 34 U.S. dollars.[5]

Maureen was traumatized by her decision to send Jayne overseas to live with people she had never met. But like most parents who decided similar fates for their children, Maureen anticipated that the war would come to a quick conclusion, perhaps in just a few months. Clinging to that hope, Maureen lovingly packed Jayne's trunk with clean and neatly pressed clothing, including a new skirt and sweater. She wanted Jayne to look her best in big, fancy America.

The night before Jayne's departure, nobody slept well. Jayne was frightened, Maureen felt sick, and Adj was worried about both of them. Compounding the stress was the heat. August had been unusually hot and sticky, and even though the windows of Adj's flat were wide open, there was no cooling nighttime breeze. And because London remained under a blackout and curfew, the city

---

[5.] The value of $34 in 1940 equals approximately $530 today.

seemed scared, too. Maureen thought, "*This is the worst night of my life.*" She perspired profusely in spite of an electric fan that whirred by her bedside.

By 6:00 the next morning, the sun already felt hot. Adj had risen early and prepared tea and toast. Maureen didn't eat. She felt tired and weak, and she was haunted by thoughts that this was the last morning she would ever see her daughter. She told herself that she was worrying unnecessarily, but how could she not contemplate the dangers? Even if Jayne's ship crossed the Atlantic safely, would she and Adj survive the German bombs?

Maureen put on a happy face for Jayne, but Jayne knew her mother was worried. She hugged her and assured her that everything would work out. Adj, too, was emotionally drained. During the weeks that Jayne had lived with her in Brighton and now in London, she had come to love her like a daughter.

The *Boston Evening Transcript* had compiled a detailed itinerary for departure day. It first instructed that Jayne and her parents arrive at London's Grosvenor House Hotel by 9:00 a.m. The hotel was the initial staging point for the 500 *Transcript* evacuees.[6]

After breakfast, Adj, Maureen, and Jayne boarded a taxi for the hotel. Jayne's trunk was placed in the taxi's boot. At the hotel, they proceeded to the opulent grand ballroom, where they met the other *Transcript* evacuees and their families. They were also introduced to the adult escort who would look after Jayne and the other children during the voyage.

Everyone was seated. A lady, probably a representative of the shipping line, gave an overview of the transatlantic crossing. Jayne learned that the name of the ship was the S.S. *Samaria* and that

---

[6.] The hotel was built on the site of the former Grosvenor House, one of the largest private homes in London, in the exclusive Park Lane district of Mayfair. The Grosvenor family (better known as the Dukes of Westminster) resided there for more than a century. After World War I, the home was sold and razed for the construction of the hotel, which remains today.

they would depart from the port at Liverpool.[7] There would be 210 children on board, along with a thousand or more adult passengers. From the Grosvenor House Hotel they would board buses for Paddington Station and then the train for Liverpool. Goodbyes must be said now. Parents and family would not be permitted to accompany the children on the buses to Paddington or on the train to Liverpool.

A man who had been seated off to the side was then asked to come forward and address the assemblage. This frail, elderly man carefully rose from his chair and shuffled forward, using a cane to keep his balance. When he reached the front of the room, he turned to face the group, pulled notepaper from his breast pocket, unfolded it, and cleared his throat.

After a few moments of studying the paper, he spoke, his eyes still focused on his notes.

He began, "The natural yearning of the human spirit is to be free." His voice was raspy and soft, yet clear. "To be free to live as you desire, worship as you so choose, and to determine your own destiny. And when these freedoms are threatened, men of faith and conscience will fight to protect them. They will even die for these freedoms. It has been this way throughout history."

Then he looked up.

"War is coming to London. I have seen war, and I know that it is something young children should never have to endure. That is why your parents strongly believe it is best that you leave England, just for awhile. You are going to sail to a place that embodies all of the freedoms necessary for you to prosper as a child. It is a place that is untroubled by the threat of war, filled with goodness, and ready to give you a childhood that the sons and daughters of freedom-loving people deserve. This place is the United States of America."

The man reached into his coat pocket, removed a small booklet, and held it high above his head.

---

7. The name "Samaria" was derived from the city of Samaria, which had been the capital of the ancient Kingdom of Israel.

"This book will help you understand the history of freedom and why it is so important. Keep it with you at all times. Read it, and learn the wisdom of its words. And when you return to England, an England that has been rid of those who threaten its existence, you will understand the fact that freedom is never free. It must be guarded and fought for at all times. This is my message to you as you embark on your journey."

The room was silent as the man shuffled back to his chair. Then copies of the same book that the man had held above his head were distributed to the evacuees. The small paperback booklet of 60 pages was titled *This Token of Freedom*. Jayne thumbed through the chapters. They were titled, "The Free People", "Patriotism and Service", "Freedom", and "Faith and Patience". Each chapter included statements, poems, and quotations from historically significant documents and figures such as the Magna Carta, Queen Elizabeth, Abraham Lincoln, William Wordsworth, William Shakespeare, Oliver Wendell Holmes, and John Milton. All words pertained to the natural yearning of the human spirit for freedom and how those who threaten it (in this case, Germany) shall be fought and defeated.

On the first page, Jayne read this personalized inscription:

> *THIS TOKEN OF FREEDOM was given to me, Jayne Jaffé, when I was 9 years old by someone who loves these words and knew what they meant and knew why I must cherish them and hold them sacred so long as I live.*

On the next page was a letter to the evacuees.

*Foreword to the Children*

> *When you see the Statue of Liberty in New York's Harbour, remember why she is holding up a light. It is what any brave Mother would do, if her children were traveling a dangerous road in what Chaucer called "the dark darkness" of this world.*

*The spirit of Freedom is so dear to the Free People that they made her image enormous, strong as bronze, beautiful as a proud young Mother.*

*Remember, too, why she is holding fast to written words in a book. MILTON tells you why, on page 33. Tyrants hate the very words Liberty, Freedom, and try to destroy the very stones on which they find such words lovingly carved.*

*But your British father and mother are saying NO to that. They have said that the name and praise of Freedom shall not be torn down and mocked. They mean what they say. And you are their Messengers.*

*You are going, for a little while, to a country where every child learns by heart at least one of the things in this book: the words of LINCOLN at Gettysburg (page 19). They are grown-up words about a grown-up Idea. But they are a Token that we Americans, like you, have been dedicated to the great task remaining before us: that we too say that the things our fathers fought for shall not perish from the earth.*

*BLW, An American in England.*

The process of saying goodbye at the Grosvenor House Hotel was a desperate moment for most parents, creating a chaotic scene of weeping, moans, and organizers shouting instructions. Fathers and mothers kissed their children again and again.

On the other hand, the children did not seem as emotionally moved; many were happy and looking forward to their great adventure. They were going on a big ship, they were going to America, and they would have stately homes, fancy cars, horses to ride, and plentiful food! The world seemed like a wonderful place.

Jayne felt her mother's tight grip as they walked hand in hand from the hotel to the boarding queue for the bus. Maureen wished the wait would just be over with and that Jayne was onboard and gone. Not that she relished their pending separation – far from it. But every second they spent together was another second to think about the decision that she had made and to fight off the demons that were telling her to reconsider.

When they reached the door of the bus, Jayne felt her mother's hand let go. There Maureen handed the escort Jayne's passport, ticket of passage, and permission papers from both England and America. The escort fumbled through them, looked at Maureen, and nodded.

Maureen hugged Jayne, kissed her on the cheek, and then took one last look at her daughter: her brunette hair neatly combed and falling just below her shoulders, white socks and polished black shoes, a knee-length cotton skirt, and top buttoned all the way up. Both of Jayne's hands clutched the handle of a small leather travel bag, over which hung a light wool coat. Maureen's heart and mind were tormented by the thought: "*Is this really the right thing to do?*"

The escort put his hand on Maureen's shoulder and said, "Ma'am?" Maureen and Jayne hugged again, and when they let go, Jayne smiled at her and said, "Goodbye, Mummy. It will be all right."

Maureen stepped back and watched Jayne enter the bus. She was proud of Jayne, who seemed calm and accepting of her situation, far more so than Maureen herself. "*Maybe it will all work out after all,*" thought Maureen. She was reassured by the children laughing and waving from the bus windows.

"*Yes,*" Maureen decided, "*Jayne will be fine.*" She turned away and took a few steps. The bus' horn honked three times. Maureen wept, but she wouldn't look back. She pushed her way through the crowd of distraught parents and disappeared into the maze of urban London.

At the moment, life was not fun or fair. Maureen had just parted from her daughter, not knowing if she would ever see her again. And now the Nazis were taking aim at London.

Just one year ago, she, Jack and Jayne had been living contentedly on peaceful Jersey Island. But that was another lifetime in a very different world.

## - IV -

## *To America*

Although America was regarded as a safe haven from German aggression, the voyage to get there was considered risky. German submarines patrolling the north Atlantic had already sunk several passenger and cargo ships, taking many innocent lives.

Although evacuee ships had British Naval escorts, hostile submarines remained difficult to detect and even harder to destroy. Whether or not this weighed into Maureen's decision is not clear. If it did, she must have assessed the voyage risks as minimal against the potential danger to Jayne living amidst German bombing. Also, should England become occupied by the Nazis, the opportunities for Jayne in free America would be exceedingly better.

Maureen's thinking may have been shared by a British statesman's editorial, which appeared in the *London Times*. It read, in part:

> There are mines strewn across the ocean, submarines lying in wait to torpedo them, aircraft searching for them to blow them to pieces. Yet I can't but believe that the crime of exposing them at sea is less than the crime of keeping them at home to be the possible victims of an invading army.

There was no doubt that Jayne's ship sailed during the most dangerous time of the war. The Germans had shown little hesitation in destroying both convoy and evacuee ships. In addition to the potential of being torpedoed by a submarine, ships might strike a mine in the shallow waters near the coast.

In the months prior to Jayne's sailing date, it was common for each evacuee convoy to have an escort of at least 35 battleships. Up to 50 ships were allotted if a convoy was transporting non-human valuables, such as the Norwegian crown jewels or the treasures of Poland's state museum. Churchill was also said to have sent much of England's gold bullion out of the country for safekeeping at Fort Knox until the war was over.

But in the four-month period between June and September 1940, 144 unescorted and 73 escorted ships had been sunk by submarines. German U-boat officers called this the "happy time", when they sank ships with ease and suffered no retribution.

When Jayne's ship set out for America in early August 1940, so many naval convoy ships had been sunk that most remaining battleships were kept along the British coast to guard against invasion. By that time, even CORB and the British Admiralty admitted that there was no hope of providing effective protection. It was into these dangerous waters that Jayne's ship sailed.[8]

---

8. One month after the SS *Samaria* arrived in New York, the steam passenger ship *City of Benares* was sunk by German torpedoes at 10:30 p.m. on September 18, 1940. It sank in 30 minutes, taking the lives of 77 evacuee children, 121 crewmembers, and 134 passengers. Among the passengers who survived were Mary Cornish, an accomplished classical pianist, and James Baldwin-Webb, Member of Parliament. Eight days after the sinking, a lifeboat with 40 adults and children was sighted from the air and the occupants rescued. The *City of Benares* was the Ellermann Line's flagship, luxuriously furnished, and staffed with British crew and Indian seamen. Children who survived recall large sleeping cabins and white-gloved stewards serving magnificent meals. The sinking of the *City of Benares* effectively ended CORB overseas evacuation operations. 60 years later, a meeting was arranged between a girl survivor and a crewmember of the German U-boat that fired the torpedoes. He apologized for the sinking and claimed they didn't know children were on board. The female survivor said that "he was a perfectly nice fellow."

The *Samaria* had recently been retrofitted as a troop ship, and her passenger capacity was increased to 2,200 persons. At 624 feet and 19,602 gross tons, she was considered a smaller class transatlantic vessel, and her single boiler engine could churn out a service speed of 16 knots. (By comparison, the Queen Mary was 1,019 feet long, 81,000 gross tons, and could turn out 32 knots.) Built in 1920 for the Cunard Line, she was used primarily for luxury cruising, beginning with round-the-world voyages in 1923 and 1924.

Due to a recent collision with an escort ship while steaming from Liverpool to New York, the *Samaria* had been recently repaired and overhauled. She was in the best condition since her launching, freshly painted in camouflage black and ochre, with a newly installed cannon at the stern and an anti-aircraft gun on the bridge.

Maureen was unaware of the ship's revitalized condition, but even if she was, it would not have eased her worries. German submarine captains and torpedoes did not discriminate among enemy ships. New, old, large, or small: they were all fair targets.

After departing Liverpool, the *Samaria* sailed northeast and rendezvoused with five other liners and five destroyers at tiny Rathlin Island off the tip of northern Ireland. The convoy set a westerly course for Halifax, Nova Scotia, Canada, a distance of approximately 2,800 miles. From Halifax, only Jayne's ship would continue to New York City, another 581 miles to the southwest.

In addition to the *Samaria*, other liners in the convoy were the *Duchess of York, Empress of Australia, Oronsay, Antonia, Georgic,* and *Orion.* The Royal Navy allocated a meager escort of five destroyers for the voyage, including the *Ashanti, Griffin, Watchman, Vortigern,* and the *Hurricane,* along with the Battleship HMS *Revenge.*

Jayne smoothly acclimated to the vessel that would be her home for the next 10 days. She shared a room with five other children, and together they were under the supervision of one adult escort. Escorts typically included nurses, clergymen, and Salvation Army officers. Parents often volunteered for escort duty, but CORB discouraged that, preferring escorts to be neutrally attached to their charges. In addition, sentiment in England viewed escort parents as cowardly and as "running away" from the perils that lay ahead in Britain.

Meals were ample, if not varied, and Jayne was seldom hungry. Breakfast was typically fruit, cereal, eggs, or fish, along with tea or coffee. Lunch consisted of soup, fish, and assorted meats. Dinner was similar to lunch, and sweets were allowed after every meal.

The Atlantic crossing offered a time for the children to become acquainted and prepare for their immersion into a new culture. The ship was more than a place to eat, sleep, and await arrival in New York; it became a floating classroom where the boys and girls learned that they were going to a very wonderful country unlike any other in the world.

Although many traditional and aristocratic Britons still resented the fact that America had become the premier world power, most acknowledged that it was a remarkable land of opportunity. They respected the personal freedoms and limited government of American life, and they wanted the young evacuees to recognize this as well.

On board, Jayne attended daily lessons on the virtues of freedom, and particularly American freedom. She learned about the U.S. Constitution and the three branches of American government: judicial, legislative, and executive. She had to memorize and recite Lincoln's Gettysburg Address, and a prize of 10 shillings was offered to the child who could accomplish this the most quickly.[9] Jayne was also reassured that when she arrived in America, she would be taken care of by a loving family.

Because of the threat of being torpedoed by Germans, all passengers, both children and adults, were repeatedly drilled in emergency procedures, including lifeboat exercises each morning. These drills involved running toward your assigned lifeboat and simulating an orderly boarding.

All passengers had to wear their life belts at all times except when eating or sleeping. These uncomfortable and cumbersome cork objects made the wearers look as if they had a pumpkin strapped around their chest.

---

[9.] 10 shillings was half a British pound, which in today's currency would be worth approximately $11.

To many of the children, the drills seemed unnecessary. Back in London, where everyone endured occasional German attacks, they understood the need for practice evacuations to bomb shelters and subway stations. But in the middle of the ocean, life appeared safe.

But the ship's captains knew otherwise. Watchmen scanned the seas, looking for the signature "death trail" of incoming torpedoes. Submarines were usually undetectable until their "tin fish" were fired. And because of that, four days into the voyage, nobody knew that the convoy was being closely followed by a German U-boat.

Under the water, the captain of a German submarine studied the convoy through his vessel's periscope. He was thrilled with what he saw: the ships were lightly escorted, and they sailed sufficiently apart from one another. With that wide spacing, he could sink at least one vessel and maybe even two before being detected. One ship in particular, the S.S. *Antonia,* was the closest vessel to his submarine and steaming nearly alone. Keeping his submarine about 1,000 yards abreast of the *Antonia,* he watched her for an hour, waiting to see if she, or her escorts, would close their gap. They did not.

The German captain gave orders to turn his submarine 45 degrees to the south and increase her speed to 16 knots. This would draw the sub closer to the *Antonia* while still maintaining a position just north of her. The submarine's nose was now pointed directly at the center of the *Antonia,* and the captain watched her intensely, hoping she would hold her position in between the battleships.

Onboard the *Antonia* and the other ships, passengers dozed or read books on deck chairs, or enjoyed afternoon tea in the dining room. The children ran about, exploring the ship's hidden rooms and playing hide and seek. The boats were like giant playgrounds, with exciting new discoveries to be made every day.

Underwater, now only 800 yards from the *Antonia,* the U-boat captain ordered the torpedoes to be armed and ready for firing. At 600 yards, the length of six American football fields, he calmly commanded, "Fire the first torpedo." He felt good about his chances, and he tightened his grip on the periscope handles and waited for the fireball explosion of a direct hit.

On the *Antonia,* a watchman on the bridge yelled, "Torpedo, over there!" The ship's officers turned their heads and saw nothing. The watchman grabbed the captain's arm and told him to follow the direction of his pointed finger. "Can you see it? It's right there!"

The captain eventually saw the torpedo, but there was little he could do. The torpedo was too close for the ship to take any evasive action, and the *Antonia* was already sailing at full speed. Their only hope was for a miss.

Beneath the sea, the submarine captain calculated that it would take approximately 20 seconds for the torpedo to reach its target. A crewmember counted off the seconds.

Aboard the *Antonia,* chaos erupted on the starboard deck. Passengers had spied the incoming torpedo, and terrified adults and children sprinted toward the lifeboats. The captain wired a message to the ships in his convoy: *Enemy torpedo inbound 45 degrees off starboard.* The officers tracked the torpedo's path through their binoculars. For a moment, it appeared as if it would collide with the ship's midsection, but then it veered slightly away. Seconds later, it passed just behind the *Antonia's* stern.

The submarine commander, cool and unfazed by the miss, ordered a 20-degree turn to the west. Newly positioned, he ordered the second torpedo to be fired. The captain was certain this one would reach its mark, right in the middle of the *Antonia's* starboard side, sinking her nearly instantly. His sub was fitted with the latest torpedo firing technology, a system that allowed torpedoes to be launched accurately without the need to aim the submarine itself at the target. When the second torpedo left its tube, the crewmember began counting; only 16 seconds would be needed before the *Antonia* and her passengers were sent to the bottom of the sea.

By now, the escort battleship captains had ordered their depth charges armed and ready for deployment. On full battle station alert, they steamed toward the submarine.

16 seconds had elapsed since the second torpedo was fired. Another miss. Through his periscope, the captain watched the *Antonia* continue on course. He also spied the battleships closing

their range. He slammed the handles of the periscope closed and commanded an immediate dive.

The near-sinking of the *Antonia* was a sobering reminder that the seemingly tranquil seas were a very forbidding place. The moods of the passengers became dour and worrisome. Even the children became less rambunctious. The evacuees now embraced the possibility of perishing at sea, in addition to the stress of starting a new life in a foreign land, separated from their family, friends, and country.

But Jayne, being an independent, mature, and emotionally stable girl, treated the experience as exciting and new. Onboard the ship, she made friends easily and even looked after those who were younger than she. Many evacuees were as young as four or five years old. Others were adolescents, on the verge of adulthood.

Not all the children adjusted as well as Jayne. Some became reclusive and uncooperative, angry to have been taken away from everything comfortable and familiar. Many cried nonstop day and night. Seasickness was rampant, and the ship's infirmary became overcrowded with moaning victims and reeked of vomit. Many children were so sick that in case of an emergency, they would have been unable to get themselves on deck.

Although the volunteer adults who escorted the children were typically vigilant about their supervisory duties, some were less attentive to their "charges". These chaperones spent the majority of their time in the ship's pub, giving their assigned children free reign.

The philosopher Isaiah Berlin, who sailed to America on an evacuee ship, described the unsupervised children as "swarming behind, on, in, above, below every piece of furniture and rigging. The noise was terrific."

Despite the tribulations inherent in every evacuee sailing, Jayne enjoyed the mild midsummer temperatures and sunshine, spending hours on deck with new friends, looking out at the vast north Atlantic. Seagulls had been following the *Samaria* since they left Liverpool, soaring on the updrafts of the ship's stern, waiting for trash to be tossed overboard. They seldom flapped their wings, and she wondered if the gulls would be with them all the way to

America. At night when she crawled into her small sleeping berth, there was still light in the sky.

On the morning of August 13, 1940, the destroyers left the convoy to accompany British ships that were steaming in the opposite direction, back to England. That meant the convoy was nearing North America, since German U-boats reputedly did not travel within 100 miles of the coast. (This would change when America entered the war in December 1941. After that, German submarines were often detected just off the eastern seaboard.) Jayne noticed that the adults became more chatty than usual, perhaps celebrating a safe crossing and the anticipation of stepping onto American soil.

Days later, the *Samaria* left the convoy and turned toward New York, and the remaining liners went on to Halifax, Nova Scotia.

When the *Samaria* came within sight of New York City, every child and adult was on deck, three and four people deep, attempting to catch a glimpse of the Statue of Liberty and the awesome skyline of New York City. For all of the evacuees and many of their escorts, seeing New York for the first time was an overwhelming emotional experience. Some compared the moment to how Dorothy and her traveling friends reacted when they saw the Kingdom of Oz for the first time.[10] In 1940, to a child from England, New York really *was* at the end of the yellow brick road of dreams, a place for the powerful, rich, famous, and happy.

When they disembarked, the children were greeted by waving crowds, the press seeking interviews, and camera flashbulbs. Local volunteers handed out welcome souvenirs, arranged sightseeing tours, and invited the children to parties with lavish food and entertainment. It was an overwhelming response from Americans who felt that they were finally helping the cause of Britain during their war.

---

[10.] The movie *The Wizard of Oz* premiered in 1939, the same year as *Gone with the Wind*. It was a box-office flop, and it only gained popularity with the advent of television in the late 1950s, when millions of children could view it.

The enthusiastic welcome of New Yorkers reinforced the children's preconceived notions of America being a land of excitement, promise, and wealth.

Like any foreign visitors, Jayne and the other children had to complete U.S. immigration and customs formalities at Ellis Island. In addition, she underwent a physical examination to ensure that she was free of communicable diseases, in good general health, and mentally stable. Thereafter, some of the children were met by their pre-assigned families or relatives. But most of them, like Jayne, had no idea where they would be living, or with whom. The process of placing these "wanderers" with families was highly orchestrated and often humiliating and uncomfortable.

Having completed their duties, the volunteer escorts handed over their charges to representatives of the U.S. Committee for the Care of European Children. For many children, the separation from their escorts was another emotional parting as both escorts and children had developed close bonds during the crossing. Years later, many escorts would regret losing contact with "their" children as the voyage was one of the most influential and adventurous experiences of their adult lives.

Jayne and 15 other children were then taken by train to Boston, where they were placed in an orphanage on Huntington Avenue called the New England Home for Little Wanderers.[11] Jayne stayed there for several days, mingling and interacting with "real" orphans who playfully short-sheeted her bed.

During her stay at the orphanage, Jayne had her first real exposure to American life. Since only a small minority of the British, and almost certainly none of the evacuee children, had ever met an American, most knew America through the filter of Hollywood movies. They imagined

---

[11.] The New England Home for Little Wanderers was founded in 1865 by 10 Boston area businessmen with an original goal of caring for children who had been orphaned by the Civil War. The home was not meant to become a permanent residence, but rather to serve as a way station where the children could prepare for a new life. It is still in operation today, making it the oldest agency of its kind in the nation.

a land populated with cowboys, movie stars, Indians, skyscrapers, gangsters with submachine guns, Negro waiters and porters, men smoking cigarettes in long cigarette holders, and flirtatious women who dressed in tight-fitting, glittery gowns and drank martinis. During their tours of Boston, many of the children were disappointed that Hollywood's portrayal of America was far from reality.

Nevertheless, American life was vastly different from that in England, and especially Jersey. Jayne saw women adorned in furs and diamonds, hundreds of the latest motorcars, billboards advertising tobacco and liquor, and shops displaying bountiful amounts of fruits, vegetables, and canned goods. There were big trains, airplanes flying overhead, and people who were not white-skinned. At night, she was amazed to see Boston adorned in bright lights and flashing neon. Back home, every major English city endured nighttime blackouts to hide its location from German bombers.

For the evacuees, Boston was an amusement park of entertainment. In comparison, wartime London seemed a depressing and unhappy place.

Within a week, nationwide representatives from the U.S. Committee arrived at the New England Home for Little Wanderers. There they began the process of placing the children with American families. The representatives reviewed the children's papers, which included information on family background, religion, age, and health. Every child was interviewed and asked probing questions before being selected by a city representative.

Children who were physically unattractive, disabled, or were perceived to have health issues sat for hours and witnessed their friends be chosen and then depart. Some evacuee children were never chosen, forcing the staff of the New England Home for Little Wanderers to search for willing host families.

Representing the Milwaukee, Wisconsin branch of the U.S. Committee was Mrs. William Van Dyke. Almost immediately, Mrs. Van Dyke decided that Jayne would travel with her back to Milwaukee. Then she selected four other British children: brothers John and Peter Cleaver, ages six and seven, and brothers Christopher and David Enion, ages five and six. Jayne was the only girl and the oldest of the group. She was meeting the Cleaver and Enion boys for the first time, as they had arrived on a different boat. (Later in life, Jayne speculated that she was chosen because her papers identified her as Catholic, the same religion as the family who would eventually care for her.)

Jayne and the Enion and Cleaver boys were "set aside" in a corner of the room while Mrs. Van Dyke met with a representative of the New England Home for Little Wanderers to arrange for the official transfer of the children. None of the young evacuees knew where they were headed; all they knew was that Mrs. Van Dyke seemed like a nice lady who was going to take them to a different city.

When Jayne heard that she was going to be living in Milwaukee, her first thought was "*Where in the world is Milwaukee?*" She knew of New York, Boston, Toronto, San Francisco, and Chicago, but Milwaukee was completely foreign to her. Yet Mrs. Van Dyke was gentle and personable, and Jayne decided that if everybody in Milwaukee was this nice, she'd be happy there.

While waiting, she began her first letter to her mother since arriving in the United States.

*Darling Mummy,*

*I am very happy and am having a lovely time. I hope you are OK. A great word for the Americans is "I guess that's OK." I had to go to Ellis Island and I passed right by the statue of Liberty. I could see the torch. On board ship I had fruit and cereal and eggs or fish and tea or coffee. For breakfast I had soup and fish, meats and sweet for lunch and for dinner I had soup and meat and sweet and coffee.*

*Today I am going to my real home, to Mrs. Sullivan, I go by train at 3:30 p.m. and arrive at about 6:30 p.m. the next day. There are four little boys coming too, and one of them has a trumpet and he plays it very loudly this morning and woke me up and he went on playing it all the time and he nearly drives me crazy.*

The Enion and Cleaver boys, Jayne, and Mrs. Van Dyke boarded a taxi for Boston's railroad station. In 1940, railroad transportation was still the fastest and most cost-effective way to travel across the United States. Airlines were well established, yet air travel remained expensive. Roads bisected most parts of the nation, but speed limits rarely exceeded 50 miles per hour on these narrow, two-lane highways.

Express rail service between Boston and Chicago's Union Station was offered by both the Pennsylvania and New York Central Railroad Companies. The Pennsylvania Railroad's service, the Broadway Limited, competed with New York Central's 20th Century Limited. It is likely Mrs. Van Dyke, Jayne, and the boys boarded one of these express trains to Chicago and then transferred lines to Milwaukee. Traveling at speeds up to 70 miles per hour and making only a few scheduled stops, the express train would zip the Milwaukee-bound evacuees to their destination in just over 24 hours.

During the trip, Jayne and the boys watched the American countryside pass by outside the railroad car window. There was more farmland and forests than Jayne anticipated. Wasn't most of America comprised of big cities? And where were the cowboys and Indians? These were the stereotypic, prevailing views of the day among almost all foreigners.

But already Jayne could sense that life in America was going to be different than the way the movies, books, and newspapers had portrayed it. And now she was headed to a city with a strange-sounding name to live with a family she had never met.

Onboard, Jayne continued writing her first letter to her mother.

> *Now we are on the train and Mrs. Van Dyke who is looking after us gave me a box of lollypops. It had 28 in it, and I have eaten 2. I have been given 5 comics and 4 books. We have just gone over two bridges and they were lovely big ones. Sorry I am writing so crooked and badly but the train is so jerky.*

> *I am sorry you didn't get letters sooner but I hadn't any money to get the stamps with cause it hadn't been changed, now I have 34 dollars and I didn't have to pay for the stamps because Mrs. Van Dyke gave them to me.*
>
> *Heaps and heaps of love from Jayne.*

She missed her mother. There was nobody's hand to hold, nobody to hug, and nobody in big, scary America who loved her as much as her mother did.

But all of that was about to change.

Jack and Maureen Jaffé stand outside their home on the Isle of Jersey, circa 1934.

Jack Hans Jaffé (far right) with members of the Royal Jersey Golf Club, circa 1934. Jaffé was a championship golfer who competed in tournaments throughout England.

Jayne Jaffé, age 3, in the garden of the Jaffé home on the Isle of Jersey in 1933.

Jayne Jaffé, age 5.

Jayne Jaffé and her father, Jack, pose for a photograph in St. Helier in 1936, just three years before his death.

A farmer leads Jersey cows past the Jaffé home while Jayne and her mother watch. This photo was published 70 years later in the July 29, 2004 edition of the *Jersey Evening Post*.

The city of St. Helier appears on a postcard from the 1930s. Jayne and her family lived near St. Helier during this time.

**PHONE 747**

# J. H. JAFFÉ & CO., LTD.
### Importers Agents

**10 BOND STREET,
ST. HELIER, JERSEY, C.I.**

*Maureen Jaffé*
**DIRECTOR**

Maureen Jaffé's business card identifies her as a director of her husband's company, J.H. Jaffé & Co., Ltd. The company's subsidiary, Jersey Paint and Wallpaper Company, still exists today.

Pix Boddington, Jayne's stepsister and the daughter of Jack Jaffé and his first wife, Maud.

Gathered at the Jaffé home are Jack Jaffé and Con Bonnington (standing), Pix Bonnington with Jayne on her lap, Aunt Grace Conway, and Kim Bonnington (on the grass), the son of Con and Pix. Although 20 years older than Jayne, Pix and her husband Con often visited Jersey and got along with Jayne and her family. Con affectionately referred to himself as Jayne's "big brother".

Aunt Agnes (Adj) Conway (center) with her second husband, Bernard Sterling, and her daughter, Mary, circa 1932. When Jayne and her mother evacuated Jersey in 1939, Adj hosted them at her cottage in Brighton and then at her flat in London.

This photo of a London railroad station shows soldiers arriving to defend London against the Nazi Blitzkrieg and children being sent to safe towns outside the city. In August 1939, more than 1.5 million children were transported out of London and resettled in the countryside under Operation Pied Piper.

The SS *Samaria* took Jayne and other English evacuee children to America in August 1940. Weeks later, evacuation sailings ended when the British Admiralty deemed the north Atlantic too dangerous for safe crossings due to increased German submarine patrols.

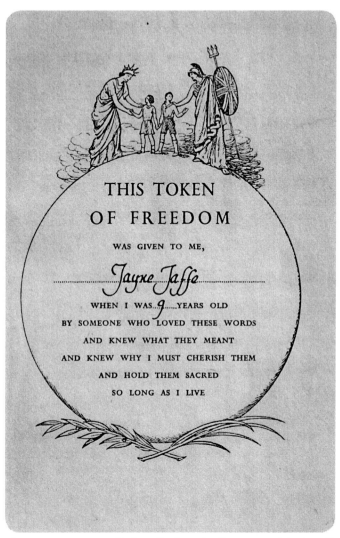

Jayne's name was personally inscribed on the first page of the handbook *This Token of Freedom*. These booklets were given to every evacuee who sailed on the SS *Samaria* from Liverpool to the United States on August 23, 1940. The booklet included quotes from famous statesmen and writers about the natural yearning of the human spirit for freedom and how those who threaten it (in this case, Germany) must be fought and defeated.

Darling Mummy

I am very happy & am having a lovely time I hope you are O.K. A great ~~for~~ word for the Americans is. I guess thats O.K. I am saying it now to. I had to go to Ellis Island which is a place ~~where~~ you have to go if you are ill, not that I was ill but I was with some one that had swolen glans & they thought she had mumps but it was OK sister, & I passed right by the statue, I could see the torch any way I came straight back again. I stayed in New York for the night

I had a lovely ice cream today & a Sugar Daddy & they were lovely they were super the ice cream was strawberry & the Daddy was treacle toffee. To day I am going to my real home, to Mrs Sullivan, I go by train. I begin at 3-30 P.M. & arrive at about 4-30 P.M. next day. I am just about to get up now, there are four little boys coming to & one of them has a trumpet and he plays it very early this morning & woke me up & he went on playing it all the time & he nearly drives me crazy

Jayne wrote her first letter to her mother while on the train from Boston to Milwaukee, almost 10 days after her arrival in the U.S.

The Chicago & Northwestern railroad station was the point of Jayne's arrival in Milwaukee on August 29, 1940. Situated along Lake Michigan, the station served as the city's major transportation center until the 1960s, when air travel became the norm.

# Five Refugee Children Arrive Here Thursday

## Little Britons Will Be Given Milwaukee Homes for Duration of War, One Family 'Adopts' Two Brothers, 6 and 7

Five British children, escaped from the terrors of German blitzkrieg, will find refuge in the homes of four Milwaukee families Thursday.

The youngsters, ranging from 5 to 11, are expected here at 11 a. m. With them will be Mrs. William D. Van Dyke Jr., member of the executive board of the Milwaukee branch, U. S. Committee for Aid to European Children. She went to Montreal to bring them here to their new homes.

Mr. and Mrs. Henry G. Wild, 5418 N. Lake dr., themselves the parents of four children, will take two of the refugees—Peter Cleaver, 7, and his brother, John, 6.

Christopher Enion, 5, will go to the home of the Jackson Bruces, 414 E. Apple Tree rd. Dr. and Mrs. A. Gledden Santer will become the war foster-parents of Christopher's brother, David. Jane Jaffey, 10, will find a playmate in Billy Sullivan, 11, son of Mr. and Mrs. Willis G. Sullivan, 5525 N. Danbury rd.

Mrs. Van Dyke will take the refugees to her home in Fox Point for lunch, after which they will be taken to their respective temporary homes.

At the station to meet them will be Maxwell Herriott, chairman of the Milwaukee executive board, and Clifford Morehouse, vice chairman.

This August 1940 article in the *Milwaukee Sentinel* announced the arrival of Jayne and the Enion and Cleaver boys. It contains three errors: Mrs. William D. Van Dyke Jr. did brought the children from Boston, not Montreal, Jayne's name is misspelled, and since the refugees arrived at 5:30 p.m., there was no lunch in Fox Point.

Willis G. Sullivan, "Uncle Bill".

Jayne and Helen Sullivan pose in the living room of the Sullivan home in Fox Point, Wisconsin. This photo was taken shortly after Jayne arrived in August 1940.

Jayne in the front yard of the Sullivan home with the Sullivan boys Bob (left) and Bill Jr. (right).

London's underground subway stations protected millions of people throughout the 56 days and nights of the German Blitzkrieg bombings in autumn 1940. The combined body heat of those seeking refuge made the shelters uncomfortably hot and stuffy.

During the Battle of Britain, Londoners were implored to "keep calm and carry on". This shopkeeper writes that he's open for "business as usual" despite the surrounding destruction.

During the Blitzkrieg, many children endured the death of family and friends. Scenes like this were a reminder of why parents like Maureen sent their children overseas for the duration of WWII.

The D-Day invasion to liberate Europe was launched on June 6, 1944. It included more than 6,000 ships of all kinds (forming the largest armada in history), 326,000 troops, nearly 12,000 aircraft, 54,000 vehicles including tanks, and more than 106,000 tons of supplies.

Winston Churchill, Franklin Delano Roosevelt, and Joseph Stalin gathered in February 1945 at the Yalta conference in the Crimea, Ukraine. These men led the nations at the core of the Allied forces that defeated Germany. After the war, Stalin and the Soviets would impose Communist dictatorship on much of Europe, including Poland, Czechoslovakia, Romania, and Hungary.

The French liner SS *Ile de France* carried Jayne and other evacuee children back to England after the conclusion of WWII. Decorated entirely in the art deco style, it was considered one of the most beautifully appointed ships of the time.

12A. Clarendon Court
London. W. 9.
13-10-47.

Dear Mr. Sullivan,

First of all, I want to thank you for offering to help us get settled in Milwaukee. As you know, no other part of the U.S. counts to Jayne, and she's been pining to get back ever since she left, – and I realize now that she will never feel really at home over here.

We went to the American Consulate last week and got the necessary forms. Amazingly enough, there seem to be no quota difficulties for British people, but it is necessary to have sponsors and guaranteed employment.

Now, I don't know quite what

In her letter to Bill Sullivan on October 14, 1947, Maureen acknowledges Jayne's desire to return to Milwaukee.

The flagship of the Cunard Line, the *Queen Mary*, arrives in New York with soldiers returning from Europe. Jayne and Maureen sailed on the *Queen Mary* when they came to the U.S. in April 1948. At that time, the ship, still painted camouflage gray, was affectionately referred to as the "Gray Ghost".

Jayne, age 17, shortly after her return to the Sullivan home with her mother in 1948. The girl in the photo is the photographer's daughter.

## - V -

## *Where in the World Is Wisconsin?*

When Willis G. Sullivan of Fox Point, Wisconsin read about the young British evacuees coming to America, he knew immediately that he wanted his family to host one or more of the children. Not only would he be "doing his part" to help the British war effort, but having a surrogate child from England would be a good experience for his family, especially his two sons, Bob and Bill Jr., ages 9 and 10. His wife Helen agreed, and they notified the Milwaukee branch of the U.S. Committee for the Care of European Children.

Willis Sullivan was a successful Milwaukee attorney and partner in the firm Sullivan-Lauritzen, Ltd. His wife Helen had responsibilities typical of wives of the era: looking after the children, cooking, cleaning, and keeping the Sullivan home in good operational order.

After interviewing with representatives of the Milwaukee branch of the U.S. Committee, the Sullivans were deemed an acceptable host family, along with two other couples. When given the names and ages of the children who were to arrive with Mrs. Van Dyke, the Sullivans were disappointed that a young girl, perhaps three or four years old, was not among them. They theorized that a younger girl, still in her earliest formative years, would be less challenged to adjust to life away from England. They also suspected that their two sons would more easily adapt to a younger girl as opposed to one their own age.

In the end, the Sullivans had no choice but to select nine-year-old Jayne Jaffé. The next day, an article in the *Milwaukee Journal* announced that "Five British children, escaped from the terrors of German blitzkrieg, will find refuge in the homes of four Milwaukee families Thursday."

Jayne's train was scheduled to arrive in Milwaukee on August 29, 1940. In advance of that day, Willis Sullivan made certain that the family home was prepared. He personally mowed the lawn and trimmed the bushes. Helen cleaned the house and stocked the refrigerator and pantry with food. Bill Jr. and Bob washed the family car, a new 1940 Ford sedan with four doors, wide whitewall tires, and a Motorola radio. The entire family made a large sign and hung it in the entry foyer. It read, "Welcome to America Jayne" and had a U.S. and a British flag drawn beneath the letters. It was a grand preparation to welcome a nine-year-old girl about who the Sullivans knew little other than her name.

That night, the Sullivans slept poorly. Bill worried that he had made a poor decision in accepting an English refugee. What if she was ill-mannered and didn't fit into his family? Helen was concerned about raising a surrogate daughter. She was only familiar with mothering boys and knew very little about the needs of a young girl. The boys didn't like the idea of having any girls in the house at all.

After the sun rose on the humid morning of Thursday, August 29, the family gathered around the breakfast table. Bill told his family that this day was going to be meaningful and memorable. He reminded everyone why Jayne was coming to live with them. England was suffering in ways that Americans could not fully understand. Bombs were falling in London and people were dying, even young boys and girls. Food was rationed. And the entire nation could be occupied by the dictatorial and brutal Nazis.

Helen and the boys listened to him silently, occasionally nodding. Bill ended by saying, "Jayne is going to be a part of our family. We will love her like a daughter and a sister."

As the boys finished their eggs, bacon, and toast and asked to be excused, Helen looked at her husband. Bill nodded and told the boys, "We leave to get Jayne at 5 this afternoon. Dress in your white shirts, knickers, and best shoes. And before we go, take a bath."

The boys groaned and rolled their eyes, then grabbed their baseball mitts and ball and went outside.

That afternoon, everyone boarded the family sedan and left for the Chicago & Northwestern Railroad Station on Milwaukee's lakefront. The boys were dressed as their father had instructed, with their hair combed back and held in place with a creamy tonic. Helen wore a maroon summer blouse, a cream colored, lightweight cotton skirt that fell just below the knees, stockings, and heels. Bill wore his white summer sport coat and a dark tie, khaki trousers, and shiny white buck shoes.

The route to the Chicago & Northwestern Railway Station, located in downtown Milwaukee, followed a fashionable street named Lake Drive, just a block away from the Sullivan home. Along this road, the Sullivans traveled south through the suburbs of Fox Point and Whitefish Bay, with their luxurious brick and stone homes and manicured lawns. Large elm trees shaded the homes and formed a tunnel-like roof over the road, offering a cooling sanctuary from the hot August sun.

Lake Drive turned east toward Lake Michigan and followed the shoreline past wide sand beaches teeming with sunbathers and swimmers. There was also the Milwaukee Yacht Club, with hundreds of expensive boats moored in their slips. Bill and Helen treasured this part of Milwaukee, for it gave the city a cosmopolitan appeal, and if one didn't know better, you could mistake this maritime environment for the coast of California or even Florida.

In the back seat, the boys tried to stay cool by hanging their arms from the windows. Bill rolled up his shirt sleeves, and Helen dabbed her forehead with a handkerchief.

"I hope Jayne is dressed for this heat," Bill commented. "They seldom have hot weather in England, seeing as it's one big island in the cool north Atlantic ocean." He cranked down his window a little further.

The railroad station, a red brick, Romanesque style building, stood at the terminus of Lake Drive. It was the transportation hub of Milwaukee, and railroad cars, both freight and passenger, sat on an expanse of tracks so wide that they nearly reached Lake Michigan. Steam billowed from engines poised to depart, and passengers hustled to and from the trains, some accompanied by black porters dressed in suits, bowties, and little white caps, who carried their luggage.

Bill parked the car, and the family entered the main hall of the depot, a cavernous room that echoed with passenger chatter, railroad conductor announcements, and the shuffle of feet. They were greeted by Mr. and Mrs. Henry Wild (foster parents of the Cleaver Boys), Mr. and Mrs. Jackson Bruce (foster parents of Christopher Enion), and Dr. and Mrs. Oscar Sandar (foster parents of David Enion). There were also newspaper reporters, photographers, and curious onlookers.

The large clock on the wall read 6:10 p.m., 20 minutes before Jayne's train was due to arrive. Bill asked Henry Wild if it was on time, and he shook his head. "She's going to be early today, Bill. We should hear her whistle any moment now."

Bill's stomach knotted. Helen, still nervous about having to raise a girl, cooled her face with a small oriental style fan. The boys stood still while Bill adjusted their shirts and knickers.

A train horn sounded, and through the loudspeaker a man's voice announced, "Hiawatha Express #446 from Chicago is now arriving on track 2. Passengers will enter the station through the door marked track 2."

A black steam engine pulling about a dozen coach cars hissed and huffed into the station and stopped. Through the windows, the Sullivans watched the conductors trot to the train carrying little stools, which they positioned beneath the railcar doors. When the ladies disembarked, the conductors extended their hands to help them. When the men exited, they held their hands just beside their shoulders to catch them should they stumble.

Bill and Helen stood on their toes and peered over the crowd, looking for Mrs. Van Dyke and the refugee children. They saw businessmen in suits and hats, parents with their children, and ladies carrying shopping bags in each hand. Conversation among the foster parents was repetitive. "Do you see them? No! Do you see them? No, I don't see them. Do you?"

"Perhaps they never got on this train," Helen speculated. The boys smiled at each other, happy at the thought. Oscar Sander, one of the foster fathers, nudged Bill. "Look there!" He pointed to the front of the train, and Bill saw Mrs. Van Dyke holding the hand of a small girl, with four boys following them.

The foster parents went to the door marked track 2 and unintentionally spread out in a semi-circle, shoulder to shoulder. Mrs. Van Dyke and the children entered the station and stopped several feet from the families. There was an awkward moment of silence until Bill stepped forward, walked over to Jayne, and bent down with his hands on his knees so his eyes met hers. He extended his hand. "So, you must be Jayne. I'm your Uncle Bill. Welcome to Milwaukee. We're very happy that you're here."

Jayne smiled, and instead of shaking Uncle Bill's hand, she curtsied and said, "Thank you, sir."

The boys snickered at her British accent.

The two sets of refugee boys were indistinguishable from each other, so Mrs. Van Dyke introduced them to their foster parents. The boys shook hands with their eyes cast downward.

There was paperwork to complete, but Mrs. Van Dyke claimed that could happen over the weekend. For now, everyone should go home and settle in. She hugged every one of the children and told them she would see them soon.

Uncle Bill turned to his sons and said, "Boys, would you please carry Jayne's bag?" Neither Bill nor Bob stepped forward, so Jayne said, "I can carry it. It's no trouble at all."

"I'll take it for you," Bob said. He grabbed the handle of Jayne's bag, and the entire Sullivan family, with their new daughter, left the depot for home.

After a month of wondering, Jayne had finally met her American family. It was a relief that they seemed so kind. She had worried that they would be mean or rude because it was rumored that some Americans were like that. But as they walked to the car, Aunt Helen placed a reassuring hand on her shoulder, and Uncle Bill kept welcoming her to his family. Even the boys seemed well-mannered, at least for boys.

Across the Atlantic, in London, Maureen lay in bed listening to the 10 p.m. radio news from the British Broadcasting Corporation. Most of it was grim. Hitler's German war machine continued its occupation of most of Europe and now Norway. Only England remained to be conquered, and Germany was preparing to destroy London. The American ambassador to England, Joseph Kennedy, had advised Americans to leave the country. Prime Minister Churchill addressed the British people, stating that the entire future of Western civilization rested upon the successful defense of the British homeland against the Nazis.

But this news didn't interest Maureen. What she really wanted to know was the whereabouts of her daughter.

\* \* \*

In 1845, 95 years before Jayne arrived in Wisconsin, the last of the American Indians departed the region now named Fox Point. Situated along the western shore of Lake Michigan, the area's fertile soils, thick forests, and pristine waters had sustained the Potawatomi tribe for centuries.

By 1910, the Indians were gone. Fox Point was comprised of a few large homes, summer cottages, and farms belonging to descendents of European immigrants who had settled Milwaukee, a large city 10 miles to the south. Milwaukee was an Indian word meaning "gathering of waters", and to the residents of this city, built upon the confluence of the Kinnickinic, Milwaukee, and Menomonee Rivers, Fox Point was a faraway place, still wild and untamed.

By the 1940s, Fox Point was a thriving Milwaukee suburb. Jayne saw impressive brick and stone residences on quiet tree-lined lanes surrounded by wooded areas, deep ravines, and panoramic Lake Michigan vistas. The late summer sun cast long shadows, and occasionally the scent of roasted corn on the cob wafted from backyard barbeque grills.

But in the front seat of the Sullivans' Ford, seated between Uncle Bill and Helen, Jayne felt ill. She hadn't slept well on the overnight train to Milwaukee from Boston, and it was past dinner time, so she was hungry. The breeze from the open car windows seemed to reach everybody in the car except her. And the Sullivans, trying to make her feel welcome, continually pointed out the local sights and asked her questions about England. When they arrived at the Sullivan home on East Thorne Lane, Jayne only wanted to eat, and then go to sleep.

Instead, Jayne saw balloons and streamers outside of the house, and when Uncle Bill unlocked the front door there was the "Welcome to America Jayne" sign. Helen showed Jayne to her second floor bedroom, and Bob carried her bag. It was a large, private room with a sitting chair, dresser, closet, and a window overlooking the back yard. It was almost as big as the two bedrooms in Adj's London flat combined. Jayne said, "It's very beautiful, ma'am. Thank you." Helen replied that from now on, she was "Aunt Helen". "Yes, ma'am," Jayne replied, then corrected herself: "Yes, Aunt Helen." Everyone laughed, even Bob.

Aunt Helen told Jayne that the evening meal would be a summer barbeque. "That's an American thing," Bob explained. There would be grilled steaks smothered in fried onions and mushrooms, baked potatoes, fresh green salad, and lemonade. It would all be ready in about an hour. Until then, Jayne could unpack and freshen up. Aunt Helen opened the bedroom window, allowing a warm summer breeze to freshen the room, and then she left.

Jayne was too tired to unpack. She took off her warm clothes, put on a lightweight shirt and skirt, and sat down on the bed. When Uncle Bill went to get her for dinner, he found her fast asleep. He covered her with a blanket and let her sleep until morning.

\* \* \*

Jayne arrived with all of the $34 that her mother had given her, but she lacked her passport, immigration papers, visa, and medical history report. Concerned that Jayne had lost the items or that they were being held in safekeeping elsewhere, Mr. Sullivan wrote to the New England Home for Little Wanderers requesting that the missing documents be sent to him. In that letter, dated August 31, 1940, he added that "I am rather concerned about the sketchy information we have concerning this girl and her relatives."

It was clear to the Sullivans that Jayne was a pleasant and emotionally well-adjusted girl, but assessing her physical health was another matter. Although Jayne arrived with a medical report from the examining doctor upon her arrival in Boston, the information was superficial, indicating that Jayne's nourishment and development was "fair", her pupils were "equal", teeth "good", and pulse "strong". Her arrival weight was listed as 71½ pounds, and height at 4 feet, 9 inches.

The Sullivans wanted a complete medical history in case Jayne should take ill. For example, they wondered whether she had any allergies to certain medications, whether she'd had any serious illness as an infant, or whether she had ever been hospitalized. Jayne was of little help in offering information, as she had no memory of the years before age four or five.

In addition, the Fox Point school that Jayne was to attend required a complete medical history, including whether or not Jayne had had any diseases such as mumps, whooping cough, rickets, or measles. Also needed was verification of immunization against smallpox, diphtheria, and scarlet fever.

Mr. Sullivan wrote to Jayne's mother seeking that information. The letter, dated September 6, 1940, also read, in part,

> Do you wish Jayne to receive an Iodine Tablet once a week during the school year in order to prevent the development of a goiter? This procedure is recommended by the State Board of Health in the prevention of Simple Goiter. Iodine in small doses is here offered as a food, not a medicine, to

*overcome the natural lack of iodine in the food stuffs raised in this locality.*

*As a precautionary measure, I wish you would send us a letter in which you, as the sole surviving parent of Jayne, authorize either Mrs. Sullivan or myself to consent to the performance of such surgery or rendition of such other medical attention to Jayne as in our opinion may be necessary. I make this request for the reason that our doctors are extremely reluctant to do any work on a child without the parent's consent, and should the occasion ever arise, I would not want the proper care of Jayne delayed merely because the doctor feels that he does not have the proper consent to do the necessary work.*

*Very truly yours,*
*W.G. Sullivan*

Six weeks later, an answer arrived, dated October 12, 1940. It was the first communication the Sullivans had received from Jayne's mother.

*Dear Mr. Sullivan,*

*Have just received your letter re Jayne's medical history and am enclosing a letter giving you full authority to act, on my behalf, as you would do in the case of your own children.*

*The only illness Jayne has had is whooping cough about five years ago. Also, she has had her tonsils and adenoids removed. I had her thoroughly examined by a Harley Street children's Specialist and he passed her as completely fit. She has had neither tests nor inoculations.*

*I would like to say how much I appreciate the very great kindness of you and Mrs. Sullivan in taking Jayne into your*

> family. Needless to say it has left a frightful gap in my life but I am so happy to know she has found a happy home away from this troubled country.
>
> Yours very sincerely,
> Maureen Jaffé /s/

Like many foster parents, Bill and Helen considered their little British refugee to be somewhat of a celebrity, and they proudly introduced her to neighbors and family. Their friends bought her clothing, and a dentist offered his services at no cost. Mr. Sullivan even took her to his law office, where the attorneys and staff welcomed Jayne and gave her small gifts. Essentially Jayne became their surrogate daughter, and she received all the attention and affection befitting the youngest child and only girl in the family.

For the Sullivan boys, Jayne's arrival was an intrusion into their stable family life, not something they celebrated. These feelings were not unusual among the children of American foster families. One American son later remembered,

> I asked my mother who they were and why they were here, and she just said they were war guests and they were going to stay with us for a long time. I can tell you, that didn't make me happy! I had to share things with these strangers, and couldn't even understand a word they said!

Bill Sullivan Jr., who was almost two years older than Jayne, especially resented the attention given to her, which made him feel less important to his parents. Although he remained cordial to Jayne, Bill seldom included her in his activities and did not make her feel welcome or at ease.

Bob, who was the same age as Jayne, was friendlier and often helped her adjust to her new way of life. There was much for Jayne to learn about America and Milwaukee, and she tried to absorb as much as she could to fit in more quickly. She ate new foods such as corn on the cob, peanut butter and jelly, marshmallows, pumpkin pie, waffles, maple syrup, and popsicles. Bob taught her new vocabulary, including words like *sidewalks*, *streetcars*, and *bubblers* (the Milwaukee term for drinking fountains) and slang terms such as *cute*, *guys*, and *swell*.

Also, Jayne discovered that Americans used different nouns to identify common things. For example, "Father Christmas" was called Santa Claus, "lorries" were trucks, the top of a car was called a hood, not a "bonnet", and cigarettes were called cigarettes or smokes, not "fags".

Personal hygiene was different, too. In the 1930s, even prosperous families in England usually queued to use a single family bathroom and bathed and put on clean clothes only once per week. In America, everybody smelled clean and fresh and took "showers" almost daily. Jayne was amazed that the Sullivan home had three indoor bathrooms. (Only many years later did the British and most other Europeans begin to lavish themselves with soaps, cosmetics, and frequent bathing.)

With all of the newness and excitement of America, it was easy for Jayne, and most Americans, to forget that Britain was suffering greatly. The timing of Jayne's departure was fortuitous, as within days after she set sail, the Germans took the war to London. Beginning on September 7, 1940, the first wave of German bombers, some 300 of them, escorted by 600 fighter aircraft, followed the River Thames to London and dropped thousands of tons of bombs, essentially setting the city afire. Flames engulfed warehouses, homes, and factories, and when night fell, the flames guided German pilots returning with more bombs. In his autobiography, Winston Churchill wrote:

> For fifty-seven nights the bombing of London was unceasing . . . Never before was so wide an expanse of houses subjected to such bombardment or so many families required to face its problems and its terrors.

When it was over, nearly 20,000 Londoners had died in the blitz, and nearly everyone had lost at least one friend or relative. The streets were piles of rubble. Broadcast journalist and newsman

Edward R. Murrow transmitted live radio reports from London during the attacks, and his poignant descriptions of the air raids transfixed Americans to their radios and fomented hatred for the ruthless Germans. Millions, including the Sullivans, listened to his reports broadcast from the London CBS studios.

Although most Americans were aghast at Germany's assault on England, few were ready to send troops to help her. But Murrow, like other American reporters living in London, had grown to empathize with the British cause and supported direct military involvement. He was not a correspondent who reported from the battlefield; instead, he and his wife Janet lived in central London, the bull's-eye of the Luftwaffe bombings. They had lost friends and colleagues in those raids, and because of their intimacy with London and her people, the Murrows, over time, identified more with England than with America.

Churchill knew that Murrow was a powerful mouthpiece in helping to sway American public opinion to enter the war and shrewdly brought him, along with American ambassador to Britain, Gil Winant, into his small circle of confidants. Churchill desperately needed America to help defeat the Nazis. Although the Lend-Lease program was providing England with funds and equipment, only soldiers with "boots on the ground" would bring victory in the end.[12] Yet in 1941, most Americans, including most U.S. congressmen, were strongly isolationist. Neither had the desire to declare war on Germany.

---

12. Under the Lend-Lease Act, the U.S. supplied Britain with ships, tanks, jeeps, and armament, with the provision that the surviving material would be returned at the war's conclusion. It was a decisive step away from the non-interventionist policy that had dominated U.S. foreign relations since the end of World War I. Despite the struggles of Britain against the advancing Nazis, only half of the American population supported intervention. Lobbying for increased public approval, President Roosevelt explained that his plan was comparable to someone lending a garden hose to a neighbor to put out a fire in his home. "What do I do in such a crisis?" the president asked at a press conference. "I don't say . . . 'Neighbor, my garden hose cost me $15; you have to pay me $15 for it.' . . . I don't want $15 – I want my garden hose back after the fire is over."

Even if he had never met Churchill, Morrow would still have been Britain's most persuasive proponent of American military involvement. For all of his pleasures in dining and drinking with Britain's rich and powerful, it was the middle-class working people, like Maureen, for whom he had the most affection. Those people who bore the brunt of the Blitz – "the little people who live in those little houses, who have no uniforms, who get no decorations for bravery", but who were "exceedingly brave, tough, and prudent".

Murrow gave people an idea of what things looked like, smelled like, and burned like. He made them feel like they themselves were on the streets of London. And that is exactly how Churchill wanted the American citizens and politicians, living in their own cubicles of comfort, to feel.

In one report, Murrow described rescue workers tunneling through wreckage, lifting out the dead, "looking like broken, castaway, dust-covered dolls". In another report he described the common folk, the "unsung heroes" he admired most, who went about their work with bombs falling all around them – "those black-faced men with bloodshot eyes fighting fires, the girls who cradle the steering wheel of an ambulance in their arms, or the policeman who guards over that unexploded bomb."

Murrow loved how the British responded during their most terrible hour. Like Maureen and Adj, they were steady, never panicked, and seldom emotional. Would Americans react with the same fortitude and resolve under similar circumstances? It had been more than 80 years since the United States had experienced the horror of war fought on their soil, and by 1940, veterans of the Civil War were few. And as much as he respected the United States, Murrow and other American newsmen began to resent the fact that the U.S. was content to be a spectator while London was close to annihilation.

The Blitzkrieg upon which Murrow reported began the historic Battle of Britain, which Prime Minister Winston Churchill defined as Britain's "finest hour". Facing a well-established German war machine, and against tremendous odds, England was defended by young, inexperienced fighter pilots taking to the skies to fend off

German bombers and engage in dogfights with superior German fighter aircraft. The Royal Air Force (RAF) suffered staggering casualty rates, and it was not unusual for 50 percent of British fighter airmen to be shot down during a sortie by more experienced German combat pilots.

Polish fighter pilots, fighting for England, fared better. Having escaped Poland after the German occupation, they came to Britain via dangerous and circuitous routes to help defeat the Nazis with the anticipation of returning to a liberated homeland after the war. The Poles were superb and experienced pilots, fearless and carrying a deep hatred for the savagery the German troops had levied on their motherland. Their combat record was unequaled. Churchill would later credit the Polish pilots and the RAF with his memorable and often-quoted statement: "Never in the field of human conflict was so much owed by so many to so few."

The Blitzkrieg ended the British sentiment still held by many in Parliament that "something might be worked out with Hitler". All over Europe, war drums were beating and British men were marching off to battle. Despite it all, the English still held to their "stiff upper lip" tradition. It served them well; as one Londoner expressed it in the typically understated British manner, the entire Blitzkrieg had made "things a bit awkward".

Meanwhile, the United States had not entered the war and would not do so for another 14 months. Most Americans and young British evacuees lived in a world free of stress, death, food shortages, and nightly blackouts. They received news about the suffering of the British via newspapers, newsreels shown in movie theaters, and on the radio, but still, the battles seemed far removed from their plentiful life in America.

And that was exactly the way the mothers and fathers who sent their children away hoped it would be. Parents who shipped their children out of harm's way were relieved that their sons and daughters were living an unencumbered childhood, spared from the ravages and ugliness of war.

Across the north Atlantic, most mothers and fathers, including Maureen, eagerly anticipated letters from their children but found it difficult to write themselves, as their lives were filled only with war worries and news that they did not want their children to hear. A letter from Maureen to the Sullivans seemed to carry a downcast tenor:

> *Life these days is very dreary. I do pray that this war doesn't drag on for years – it would be too ghastly.*
>
> *I am so glad Jayne has fitted in so well. She really is an awfully good child and so very loyal. She and I have had real fun together.*
>
> *Do please forgive my appalling writing but I am writing in bed as it is the only place where I can get peace and quiet.*
>
> *Best wishes to you all and thank you so much for everything.*
>
> *Yours Sincerely,*
> *Maureen Jaffé*
>
> *P.S. A big kiss for Jayne.*

Contrary to Maureen's wishes, the war did "drag on" for nearly five more years. And although the gallant British and Polish pilots who fought in the Battle of Britain had staved off a German occupation, hundreds of thousands of young British men would eventually be dispatched across the globe to halt Nazi advances and to liberate occupied nations.

Since every able-bodied British adult was expected to participate in the war effort, Maureen joined the Women's Auxiliary Air Force and was assigned duties as a telephone operator in a munitions factory. On her application, she filled out her age as 34, height of 5 feet 3 inches, and address of 16 Kensington Court, London.

Maureen and other members of the Auxiliary Air Force were affectionately referred to as "WAAFs", and they held positions deemed important for the successful execution of the war. WAAF jobs included packing parachutes, manning barrage balloons, and performing catering, meteorology, radar, transport, and communications duties. At its peak in 1943, more than 180,000 women had joined the WAAF. Working side by side with the RAF at home and overseas throughout the war, the WAAF won many honors and awards, including six military medals for "gallantry in the face of the enemy".

\* \* \*

Back in America, Jayne's first weeks in Milwaukee were a process of continual adjustment. Not only did she have to adapt to a new country and a new family, but to a new school as well.

The Sullivans enrolled Jayne in the Fox Point Elementary School, about six blocks away from their home. To ease Jayne's immersion, Bill Sullivan met with the school principal and Jayne's teacher and told them everything he knew about her, including her background, why she had come to Milwaukee, and a little bit about her personality.

On the first day of class, Bill and Helen drove Jayne to school and escorted her into the classroom. Jayne's teacher introduced her to her classmates by sharing much of the information she had learned from Bill and Helen. Since most of the children in Jayne's class had advanced through the grades together, a new student was very noticeable, and during the first weeks, Jayne's accent brought her much attention, usually in the form of teasing. Most of her classmates had never met a person from England or any other foreign nation, and Jayne was chided for the way she spoke, the brunt of mimicry and laughs.

These taunts prompted Jayne to think "*I have to lose this accent and learn to speak 'American' no matter what.*" So she set about doing just that, and within a few weeks she sounded like every other American girl.

Yet when somebody discovered that Jayne was from England, two inevitable questions were asked of her: "How do you like America?" and "Do you miss your home?"

The answer to the first question was easy. Jayne loved America. For her it was like being on a grand holiday with all of your friends. Even school was fun. And she was free of worry and need.

The second question was always awkward. Yes, she missed her mother, but even those feelings were diminishing as time passed. Beyond that, there was almost nothing that Jayne longed for across the Atlantic. But admitting that might cause others to think that England was a miserable place to live. And although that was true for the moment, Jayne had warm memories of the Isle of Jersey, Brighton, and even London before the bombs fell. Even so, she would rather be in Fox Point.

Despite the awkwardness of the first weeks of school, Jayne was, as usual, quick to make friends. LuAnne Olsen, Betty Carpenter, Nyla Norem, and Nancy Powell became her closet compatriots for the next five years, from fifth grade through their freshman year of high school at the Downer Seminary (the present site of the University of Wisconsin-Milwaukee). Teachers gravitated to Jayne as well. Irene Hildebrand, Jayne's fifth grade instructor, took a liking to her and became her school "mom" throughout her years at Fox Point Elementary School.

On warm days when Jayne wasn't in school, she and her friends would ride bikes around the neighborhood and through the local parks, or go swimming at the in-ground pool (a home luxury at that time) at the home of Ralph Evinrude. Since all of the families were members of the Fox Point Club (formerly located on Lake Drive, just north of Calumet Road), they spent weekends at the club pool and enjoyed the club grounds. Jayne took an interest in the sport of diving and even won the club diving championship in her age group.

In the winter, the girls boarded streetcars to downtown Milwaukee and watched a movie or sat at the local drugstore counter sharing ice cream sundaes or soft drinks. There was also sledding, snowmen, and snowball fights. At Christmastime there were bountiful presents, parties, sweets, and glittering Christmas trees. Bing Crosby's "White Christmas" sold more recordings than any other song in 1943 and was heard at nearly every holiday gathering.

Winters in Milwaukee were harsher than any Jayne had experienced in England. Without the moderating influence of the ocean, these winters were colder and snowier, and they seemed to last longer. But since Milwaukee is farther south in latitude, it has more daylight during the winter. At Christmastime, the length of day in London is 7 hours 50 minutes, while in Milwaukee it is 9 hours.

Like most Americans, the Sullivans prepared for the holidays with much pomp and circumstance. They selected a Christmas tree from the local lot and brought it home, where the entire family decorated it with lights, ornaments, and tinsel. There were special radio broadcasts with Christmas programming and parties with punch, cakes, and cookies. Christmas cards from friends and family arrived in the mail, sharing greetings and bits of personal news of the year.

The holiday celebrations went on while Jayne and the Sullivans watched the war in Europe with detached interest. For most Americans, the war was "over there", a conflict to be fought out between Germany and England. And although most Americans and the U.S. government empathized with the cause of the British, America had pursued an isolationist policy, retreating from direct involvement in the affairs of the warring states.

Yet Winston Churchill knew that England could not subdue Germany and Hitler on its own, nor could it liberate Nazi-occupied territory without the assistance of the United States. And although the Russians had sided with England and were heavily involved in the fighting, Churchill knew that Russian Premier Joseph Stalin was not fighting to liberate nations, but to replace Nazi occupation with Soviet Communism.

Churchill made repeated voyages to the U.S. to meet with President Franklin Delano Roosevelt and both personally apprise him of the war and ask for military involvement. Roosevelt would not commit to sending troops, as that would require a declaration of war, but the U.S. continued subtle measures to supply England with financing and, in some cases, outdated American destroyers (much to Churchill's displeasure) and other instruments of warfare.

With all the focus on Europe, Americans took less notice of Japanese imperialism. Yet the Land of the Rising Sun was on the move in the Pacific and had already invaded China and Korea, murdering millions of civilians and committing atrocities arguably more brutal than those of the Nazis. At the time, no nation in Asia could match the strength or fanaticism of the Japanese military, and Japan's commanders and Emperor Hirohito envisioned a rapid conquest of all nations as far south as Australia.

There was only one impediment to the imperialistic plans of the Japanese, and the Empire took action to remove it. On the morning of December 7, 1941, 353 Japanese fighters, bombers, and torpedo planes, launched from six aircraft carriers, initiated a surprise attack against the U.S. naval base at Pearl Harbor, Hawaii. Four Navy battleships, three cruisers, and three destroyers were sunk, and 188 aircraft were destroyed. More than 2,400 men were killed and 1,282 wounded.

The attack came as a profound shock to America and effectively ended any argument for global isolationism. The following day, the United States declared war on Japan. In his speech to the American people and a joint session of Congress, President Roosevelt described the belligerent Japanese action by using the now-famous phrase, "a date which will live in infamy".

In 24 hours, Japan's aggression had put the U.S. into a global war against Germany and Japan. Although Churchill was horrified by the news of the death and destruction wrought by the Japanese at Pearl Harbor, he was relieved that England would no longer have to fight without America by her side.

When news of Pearl Harbor broke, Jayne was staying with her friend Mary Jo Herriot and the Herriot family, as Helen and Bill Sullivan were out of town. The news dominated every radio broadcast and newspaper report and permeated conversations. All of America, in the throes of holiday merrymaking, instantly became subdued with the reality of war.

The United States, now fighting alongside Britain, would never be the same again.

\* \* \*

Thousands of American boys enlisted in the various branches of the military, eager to fight against the dastardly Japanese and the equally draconian Germans.

Throughout the winter of 1941 and 1942, America became consumed with fighting war in two theaters: the Pacific and Europe. Since the U.S. was spared from battles on its mainland, American civilians were personally removed from the terrors of warfare. Most Europeans and Asians were not so fortunate.

In London, America's entry into the war heightened the city's frantic atmosphere. In the busy central districts, American military and government personnel conscripted volumes of office space, and in some sectors, more Stars and Stripes were flying than Union Jacks. Official vehicles, escorted by police cars or motorcycles with sirens blaring, were as common as taxicabs. Restaurants added tables and staff, but even so, reservations were nearly impossible to procure. Hotel rooms were simply unavailable or unaffordable.

For Maureen and Adj, and most citizens of London, the arrival of thousands of Americans added to the stresses of living in wartime. And although the daily bombings of the Blitzkrieg had ceased, a blackout remained in effect. Every home was required to have blinds that would prevent even the tiniest bit of light from showing. Street lights remained off, and vehicle lights had to be covered by shields with narrow slits. Buses had dark blue interior lights and shading over their windows.

In a perverse way, some relished the excitement, their senses continually stimulated. Gone were the days of lazy predictability; life was like a wartime movie with action, heroes, and villains. Londoners had never experienced anything like it. Everyone was in survival mode; simply awakening alive meant you had conquered a monumental challenge, and it gave you the strength to persevere. Heavy drinking, prostitution, and extramarital affairs were no longer considered taboo; they were now accepted as necessary coping mechanisms.

As Winston Churchill's daughter, Pamela Churchill Harriman, said when it was all over, "It was a terrible war, but if you were the right age . . . and in the right place, it was spectacular."

The war affected American families as well, but in different ways.

The first major impact was that women entered the workforce, filling jobs typically held by men who had now gone to war. Attracted by good wages and benefits, females took jobs at companies that required labor to satisfy the around the clock production of military hardware. From 1941 to 1945, women comprised 36 percent of the nation's workforce, an unheard-of number for the times.

But there were consequences to the bourgeoning workforce of women. With many husbands and fathers at war, tens of thousands of children were left unsupervised through much of the day. As a result, juvenile delinquency and truancy rose dramatically.

Living in the safe cocoon of Fox Point, Jayne seldom experienced the new paradigms caused by war, and for the most part, life at the Sullivans' house seemed to go on as usual. But to do their part to help the war effort, the Sullivans and other Milwaukee families were introduced to recycling. All Americans were encouraged to salvage their tin cans, bottles, rubber items, paper, scrap metal, and even fats left over from cooking. All of these materials were needed to provide America's fighting forces with the goods they needed to win the war.

Food rationing was implemented, and although it was nowhere near as restrictive as in England, substitute foods found their way into Aunt Helen's kitchen, including dried powdered eggs, lard instead of butter, and liquid paraffin instead of cooking oil.

Many families turned their backyards into "victory gardens", as the government encouraged Americans to grow their own food. The endeavor was so successful that at one point during the war, 50 percent of the nation's vegetables were grown in victory gardens.

Even fashion was influenced by the war. The War Production Board, which oversaw the allocation of materials and production facilities, essentially halted the production of new clothing and shoes, since cotton, wool, and leather were needed for the war effort. The board also dictated that companies shift their operations to the manufacturing of war necessities.

Singer Sewing Machine Company, for example, was directed to cease production of all sewing machines. Instead, Singer made airplane navigation equipment, hydraulic and electric motor control units for airplanes, gun turret castings, aircraft engine piston rings, bomber gun sights, and machine gun parts and ammunition boxes.

Chrysler, General Motors, and Ford produced only 139 cars during the entire war. Chrysler made aircraft fuselages, and General Motors made airplane engines, guns, trucks, and tanks. Ford, at its vast Willow Run plant in Ypsilanti, Michigan, assembled the B-24 Liberator bomber. The average Ford car had 15,000 parts, and the bomber required 1,550,000 parts. Nevertheless, one bomber came off the assembly line every 63 minutes during a 24-hour production cycle.

Yet to Jayne, life at the Sullivan home and in Milwaukee seemed to go on as usual. And after months of cold and snow, everyone embraced the warmer days of summer. For the Sullivans, summer meant they could finally return to their vacation home in the lake, forest, and river country of far northern Wisconsin. There they maintained a cabin on Star Lake, near the small town of Manitowish Waters.

Jayne discovered that going "up north" was a popular summer tradition in Wisconsin. It was kind of like Londoners summering in the countryside or citizens of Paris going to the beaches of Normandy. The Sullivan boys, Bill and Bob, especially looked forward to going north, as it meant many lazy days of swimming, fishing, boating, and exploring the woods and nearby small towns.

But Jayne cringed when Uncle Bill told her "We're all going up north next week, including you, Jayne." He announced it with enthusiasm and excitement, but to Jayne, it meant a month of misery and boredom.

It wasn't that Jayne hated the north woods. She appreciated the clear lakes, the fun little towns, and the beautiful forests. But all that was overshadowed by having to leave her friends to be stuck in a small cabin with Bill and Bob, with whom she still felt uncomfortable. Further, the cabin had no indoor plumbing, so everybody used a smelly outhouse and took baths in the cool lake. To the Sullivans, this was all a grand summer adventure.

One day, Jayne spied a handsome young man briskly walking toward the cabin and waving both hands. It was Tom Hites, Jayne's boyfriend. Jayne was happy to see him, but the Sullivans were not. Nobody, including Jayne, had invited him for a visit, and so despite Tom's resourcefulness in finding the cabin and making his way there (he was staying with his family on a nearby lake), he was encouraged to leave after spending one night.

During each of her first two summers in America, Jayne endured a month at the Sullivans' Star Lake cabin. During the remaining summers, the Sullivans enrolled Jayne in a private resident camp in northern Minnesota. This, too, was in the "north woods", but it was vastly different than the Sullivan cabin.

The Minnesota camp offered exciting daily activities that included canoeing, swimming, hiking, horseback riding, crafts, and games. The camp held the ceremony of raising and lowering the American flag and reciting the Pledge of Allegiance. There were also many girls Jayne's age whom she quickly befriended. During the two months she spent at the camp (whose name she cannot recall), Jayne was free to be herself, away from the influencing dynamics of the Sullivan home. It was a very liberating experience.

Whatever the season, Jayne was living the life of a typical teenage girl in suburban Milwaukee, and her experiences were overwhelmingly positive and healthy. She had surrogate parents who loved her and cared for her, many close girlfriends, a good school, and recreational opportunities that most British children could only dream about. America was indeed an amazing place.

But not all evacuee children, or their hosts, were so fortunate. When asked about her experiences in America, one former child evacuee wrote in 2002, "For me it was such a dreadful experience, I can't ever speak of it again." It was a sentiment unfortunately shared by hundreds of other evacuees after they returned home to England.

Although CORB and the U.S. Committee attempted to place evacuee children with families who "approximated the background from which the children have come, both educationally and economically", mismatches often occurred.

For example, the sons and daughters of low-income laborers, who only knew the squalor of London's dark and sordid slums, found themselves living in the luxurious homes of wealthy white-collar suburbanites. This was a dream come true for many poor children, many of whom returned to England determined to work their way out of Britain's institutionalized class system. In America, they found that you could be whatever you wanted to be, if you were willing to work hard enough.

Conversely, children of schoolteachers, businessmen, or lawyers were placed in poor, rural America. One evacuee recalled living in a tiny shack in a mining village, sharing beds, and using a privy in a cow pasture. Others arrived to hosts who were the age of their English grandparents, couples in their sixties or seventies who quickly discovered that the challenges of caring for another child were well beyond their physical capabilities. These experiences were less impressive, and many evacuees moved from family to family until a proper match was found.

Many host families recall being horrified by evacuee children who lacked couth or proper manners. Some had never sat at tables for meals or used indoor bathrooms. Those who came from the London slums used foul language and were prone to stealing and treachery, like the pickpocket children in the novel *Oliver Twist.*

When the children finally settled into suitable homes, CORB and the U.S. Committee sent formal notification letters to their birth parents in England, including the foster parents' names and addresses. Personal letters from the foster parents usually followed, in which they described themselves, their home, daily life, hobbies, and other details that distant parents might be interested in. The children wrote home as well, reassuring, in most cases, that they were fine and enjoying themselves tremendously. Although it was true that many evacuees endured untenable living conditions and were terribly homesick, the majority, like Jayne, were beginning what they would recall as the best episodes of their lives.

Communication between Maureen and Jayne and the Sullivans was sporadic and difficult. In the early 1940s, there was no e-mail, and telephone conversations were prohibitively expensive, scratchy, and often unintelligible. In addition, most British homes were not equipped with telephones, so calls had to be placed or received at special telephone stations. Cablegrams were usually reliable, but they, too, had to be sent from special facilities that were often crowded with customers. Cablegrams were also expensive, especially for meager wartime budgets. Even traditional letters were unreliable, as wartime disruptions caused them to be lost or sunk with the ships that carried them.

Still, Jayne wrote to her friends and mother in England and Jersey. When she received a reply, the letters sometimes contained distressing news of bombings, death, and destruction. One letter from Jersey stated that German soldiers were living with them in their home and that many Jewish friends and families had been deported – to where, nobody was certain.

Although both Jayne and the Sullivans regularly wrote to Maureen, their correspondence often took months to reach England, and some letters never arrived at all. For over a month, Maureen had not heard from Jayne or the Sullivans, so she finally sent a cable on December 18, 1942 that read simply "GREETINGS TO ALL PLEASE WRITE WORRIED." Mr. Sullivan replied three days later: "JAYNE FINE LETTERS PROBABLY DELAYED OR LOST."

As the years passed, Jayne felt increasingly distant from London, her mother, and everything British. Even writing home became an uncomfortable exercise. How could Jayne share the happy news about her life in America when she knew that her mother was suffering through wartime dangers, rationing, and the absence of almost everything luxurious and fun?

But Maureen took comfort in knowing Jayne was in a world far from the horrors of London. Jayne's letters provided a happy escape from her dreary life and a way to shut it all out, at least for the moment. And although Maureen missed her daughter terribly, she was finally at peace with her decision to send her away.

It was the ultimate sacrifice she could make for the person closest to her in her life.

## - VI -

## *Back Home to England*

The war dragged on for five years. During that time, evacuee boys turned into young men, and girls into young ladies. Parents in England divorced, grew older, developed illnesses, or died in the war. The lives of parents and children had changed dramatically, and when the war ended, their reunions would be awkward and even unwelcome.

It was predetermined that evacuee children would be sent home immediately after hostilities concluded. For three of the five years Jayne lived with the Sullivans, America had been fully vested in the war effort, fighting in both Europe and the Pacific. Like most Americans, the Sullivans and Jayne followed the war via radio broadcasts and newspaper reports.

By spring of 1945, Hitler's military and most German cities had been decimated. The morale of the German people was low, and Hitler had sequestered himself in an underground Berlin bunker, where he feebly directed the final German war effort. As Russian troops closed in on Berlin, hopes were high that the war in Europe would be over. Finally Maureen could contemplate a reunion with her daughter, and she wrote an expectant letter to Helen Sullivan.

*This Token of Freedom*

*28 March, 1945*

*My dear Helen,*

*With the Germans really cracking up at last, I felt I must write to you re Jayne's return. Little did either of us think when you so generously took her in 1940 the war would still be on in 1945 and I do hope you haven't felt that it has been too long.*

*It is very difficult for me to put into words my deep gratitude to you and Mr. Sullivan — you've been so wonderful to Jayne, giving her, in addition to all the material things, that happy home background that a child should have. It has been the one bright spot for me in the dark years we've been through and I know that she will always be bound to you by the years of loving care you have given her.*

*I'm afraid Jayne is going to find things very tough over here, but we'll manage somehow. Helen dear, you would be doing us both a great kindness if you would prepare her a little for the difficulties ahead.*

*The worst of these is having no home of our own. From what I can gather, there is very little chance of any of our furniture still being in Jersey. This is pretty grim because furniture here is practically unprocurable even at fantastic prices — so much has been destroyed.*

*I will, of course, have to keep on working because it will be years before I can get any money from Jersey, if ever! So I don't want poor old Jayne to have a shock — she will be coming back to a very different world than the one she left. However, it's amazing how things work out, so it's no good worrying too much.*

*The news is really splendid and I'm sure that when the Germans are finished off, the Japs won't be able to hold out very long with our combined forces all out against them.*

*It will be very comfortable to feel when you get into bed at night that you're not likely to wake up either under a heap of rubble or in the next world!*

*So please write me a few lines as soon as you have the time and I will keep you posted re arrangement this end. My best wishes to you all.*

*Yours ever,*
*Maureen*

*P.S. Will you please give Jayne my very best love and tell her I will write to her at the week-end.*

In the spring of 1945, Russian troops entered Berlin, and Hitler committed suicide in his bunker. Shortly thereafter, in the same bunker, the wife of Hitler's chief of staff, Josef Goebbels poisoned their six young children, and then took her own life. On May 7, at 2:41 in the morning, German General Alfred Jodl signed his country's formal declaration of surrender in a small brick schoolhouse in Reims, France. When he was finished, he stood back and said, in English, "I want to say a word."

The allied generals said nothing, but Jodl continued. "With this signature, the German people and the German armed forces are, for better or worse, delivered into the victor's hands. In this war, which had lasted more than five years, both have achieved and suffered more than perhaps any other people in the world. I can only hope that the victor will treat them with generosity."

The next morning, May 8, 1945, the headline of the *Stars and Stripes*, the newspaper of the U.S. Armed Forces, read in extra-bold type, **GERMANY QUITS**.

> Today, May 8, is VE-Day (Victory in Europe) and will be officially proclaimed so by the leaders of the Big Three in simultaneous declarations in Washington, London and Moscow. This was announced last night following the unofficial celebrations yesterday afternoon through the world, inspired by a broadcast by Germany's new Foreign Minister that the Wehrmacht High Command had ordered its armed forces to surrender unconditionally.

A companion article described celebrations in New York City.

> Clouds of torn paper and ticker tape swirled down on screaming crowds packed in the streets of New York this morning within a few minutes after news had been received that Germany had surrendered unconditionally.
>
> Office girls opened windows and emptied wastebaskets. Bits of paper fluttered in clouds all over Manhattan and settled in a thick carpet on the damp streets. Some offices closed as soon as word was received from Associated Press at 9:35 a.m. and employees joined the thousands milling through the thoroughfares.
>
> City authorities said the crowds, estimated at 1,000,000 persons, were "bigger than 1918 (the year WWI ended)." The streets were knee deep in paper, all phones were dead and traffic was diverted.
>
> In the Hudson River, liners and tugs let loose their sirens, adding to the noise of planes that dipped crazily over the city.

In London, hundreds of thousands of people spilled into the streets surrounding Parliament, Trafalgar Square, and Piccadilly Circus. It was as if, one Londoner observed, the city had been "taken over by an enormous family picnic". Soldiers kissed women in the streets, church bells tolled, and tugboats on the Thames River bellowed their horns. It was a magnificent spring day, and the blue skies and warm sunshine complemented the joyous celebrations.

In Moscow, citizens shouted "We love Americans," and the Star Spangled Banner was played over loudspeakers. In Paris, cannons boomed and confetti fell from windows. The new president, Harry Truman, addressed the American people in what was the most listened-to radio broadcast ever. Never in history had half the world celebrated together on one day.

But there was still the matter of the Japanese Imperial Army and the Pacific theater of combat. The war would not be entirely over until Japan was defeated, and the Japanese were a formidable enemy, presenting military challenges not found in the European theater of operations.

Jayne learned that Japanese society had a volatile combination of feudalism and nationalism that resulted in an acceptance of military rule. The Japanese armed forces were a highly nationalistic, well-established, modern fighting force. Their doctrine was the Bushido Code of feudal Japan that glorified battle and condemned weakness. It demanded bravery, loyalty, and allegiance to orders, and it forbade surrender. In combat, the Bushido Code motivated troops into suicidal *banzai* charges and required soldiers to take their own lives if threatened with capture. Surrender was disgraceful not only to the soldier but to his entire family. Documented accounts tell of soldiers' wives committing suicide because of rumors that their husband dishonorably surrendered.[13]

---

[13.] Some Japanese soldiers held out until the 1980s, decades after Japan had been defeated. When they were discovered hiding in remote areas, they wept and refused to surrender to anyone other than their commanding officer. They also apologized for not serving his majesty satisfactorily.

President Truman was presented with two alternatives to bring the war against Japan to a conclusion. He could either authorize a massive military invasion of Japan itself or employ a new weapon, the nuclear bomb.

Together with the United Kingdom and the Republic of China, the United States called for the surrender of Japan in the Potsdam Declaration on July 26, 1945. But the Japanese government ignored this ultimatum, and by President Truman's executive order, the U.S. dropped the nuclear weapon "Little Boy" on the city of Hiroshima on Monday, August 6, 1945, followed by the detonation of "Fat Man" over Nagasaki on August 9.

Six days after the detonation over Nagasaki, on August 15, Japan announced its surrender to the Allied Powers, signing the Instrument of Surrender on September 2, officially ending the Pacific War and therefore World War II.[14]

The end of the war affected nearly every American family. More than 290,000 American boys who left their mothers, fathers, girlfriends, and buddies back home would never return. Veterans who were fortunate enough to return home were hailed as heroes. Congress passed the Servicemen's Readjustment Act (informally known as the G.I. Bill) that provided college, high school, or

---

[14.] The use of nuclear weapons to end the war was highly controversial and remains so today. Decades later, in a conversation with Paul Tibbets, the captain of the B-29 Superfortress bomber from which the Hiroshima bomb was released, Japanese fighter pilot Mitsuo Fuchida told Tibbets, "You did the right thing. You know the Japanese attitude at that time, how fanatic they were, they'd die for the Emperor. Every man, woman, and child would have resisted that invasion with sticks and stones if necessary. Can you imagine what a slaughter it would be to invade Japan? It would have been terrible. The Japanese people know more about it than the American public will ever know." Fuchida's comments gave credibility to President Truman's argument that the use of a nuclear bomb would immediately end the war and save millions of lives that would have been lost during an allied invasion of Japan.

vocational education for the returning vets. It also provided financial loan opportunities for servicemen to buy homes and start businesses and farms.

With the removal of wartime price controls, prices in Milwaukee and across the country skyrocketed. As purveyor of the household, Aunt Helen complained about the cost of keeping her family fed. Uncle Bill reminded her that at least they could buy the foods they desired. In Europe, millions of families were lucky if they saw butter and cream once per month. Jayne knew this was true but not because her mother told her. Maureen's letters seldom spoke of the discomforts endured by the citizens of London, but the movie theatre newsreels did.

For the Sullivans, the end of the miserable war meant Jayne would have to return to her mother in England. So on August 13, 1945, Bill Sullivan sent a letter to the U.S. Committee for the Care of European Children and inquired about Jayne's return passage.

A week later, he received this reply:

*Dear Mr. Sullivan:*

*We have Jayne's name on the priority list for a sailing opportunity at any time after September first. However, at this writing, we have no way of knowing exactly when this will be. We depend entirely upon the nomination of the British Ministry to the steamship company, who then notify us when there is a ship and space for the child. Immediately when we have word that there is such an opportunity for Jayne, we shall wire you. In the meantime, we would suggest that insofar as is possible you have her ready around the first of September so that it will not take too long to finish preparations for her return trip.*

*Sincerely yours,*
*[Miss] Alma R. Bloch*
*Migration Consultant*

Two weeks later, on August 31, a telegram arrived stating that Jayne was booked for passage on a ship departing from New York on September 9, 1945. Since the Sullivans were already at their Star Lake cabin, where they intended to stay through the Labor Day weekend, Mr. Sullivan immediately wrote back and stated that the "September 9 sailing date may not be acceptable." It was a bold statement to make, as the U.S. Committee was not disposed to arranging return trips at the convenience of the host families. Short of serious illness, host families were expected to make every effort to deliver their evacuee child to New York a day in advance of the assigned sailing date.

There is no written record of the U.S. Committee's negative response to Mr. Sullivan's request. Jayne's sailing date had been set, and there was no way to postpone it or to avoid the reality that Jayne was leaving.

Acknowledging this, Mr. Sullivan wrote back to the U.S. Committee.

> *Dear Madam: Re: Jayne Jaffé*
>
> *As the wires have advised you, we have completed arrangement for Jayne to arrive in New York on the* Pacemaker [the train that traveled the Milwaukee to New York City route] *on Saturday, September 8, 1945, and she will call at the Traveler's Aid desk to find her escort.*
>
> *In view of the manner in which we have had to rush preparations, we were unable to get Jayne's trunk out until this morning. It is being sent to the dock by express, and we hope it will arrive there Friday morning, as the rules of the Cunard Line require, but the express company could give us no assurance. It might be wise to have someone check on the arrival of her trunk and make sure it is on board.*
>
> *Jayne's trunk weighed 140 pounds and she will have additional luggage which she will take with her, and I*

> *assume there will be no difficulty in getting this additional luggage onto the boat. In addition, we are preparing a twenty-five pound package of food which she will have with her, and I assume the necessary arrangements can be made to get this parcel on the boat.*
>
> *Unless we hear from you to the contrary, we will assume that the passport has arrived in your office and that all necessary arrangements have been completed.*
>
> *Very truly yours,*
> *WG Sullivan*

The Sullivans cut short their Star Lake vacation and drove home immediately. Bill Sullivan took ill, and Jayne remembers that he spent most of the return drive lying down in the back seat. Aunt Helen speculated that Uncle Bill was overwrought at the thought of having to part with Jayne on short notice. With more time, he would have mentally adjusted to the family shakeup. Jayne was the surrogate daughter who he had nurtured into young adulthood. In a way, he was now experiencing what Maureen felt when she waved farewell to Jayne as she boarded the bus outside of the Grosvenor House Hotel in London. Neither knew if they would ever see Jayne again.

Maureen, all too familiar with the struggles of having to send a child away, wrote a sympathetic letter to Aunt Helen on September 9:

> *My dear Helen,*
>
> *I've just receive your letter of the 4th and although it's only Wednesday, and Jayne doesn't arrive till next Monday, I felt I must just write you a line to say how sorry I am that you had such a frightful time getting her off, and I do hope your husband hasn't had any ill effects from having to make the long journey home with such a high temperature. Also, I feel that you've probably had your summer holiday spoiled. It's*

*just too much for you to have had this final trouble after all you've done for Jayne all these years.*

*I will send you a cable as soon as Jayne arrives and write you my impressions fully. I can't tell you how grateful I am to you and all your friends whom I will write personally. You and your family are part of Jayne's life now and I know she's going to miss you all very much. It's a hasty wrench for both sides.*

*I'm glad you've been strict with her, Helen dear; girls in their teens (middle, anyway) are at their most difficult age and need a firm hand. The adjustment is bound to be a little tricky, but I hope to get over it with a bit of tact and tolerance.*

*We <u>must</u> keep in touch.*

*Tons of love to all, In haste,*

*Yours,*
*Maureen*

News of Jayne's imminent departure quickly spread through Fox Point. Her friends organized a farewell party and presented her with a silver bracelet gift from "the gang." Adults and friends stopped by the Sullivans' home to say goodbye, and Jayne received farewell cards and hugs.

The Sullivans themselves were not a tearful bunch. Helen and Bill dealt with Jayne's departure in a matter-of-fact way. It was a requirement that needed to be fulfilled and part of the deal they'd agreed to. When the war ended, Jayne would go home. It was that simple.

But they were undoubtedly bereft that the little British refugee, who had become their surrogate daughter and a welcome addition to their family, was leaving.

For the Sullivan boys, Bill and Bob, Jayne's departure was likely greeted with mixed emotions. On the one hand, they would be relieved of the interloper who had monopolized the attention of their parents. But as the years passed, their hearts had softened. They realized Jayne was a nice girl, never spiteful, mean, or vindictive. She was grateful for everything the Sullivans had given to her, and she was always polite and smiling.

For Jayne, everything was happening so suddenly that she didn't have time to feel strong emotions. Only when she arrived at the Chicago & Northwestern Railroad station along Milwaukee's lakefront did the tears begin. There, in the station's cavernous main hall, she looked at the entire Sullivan family, her friends, and some of their parents and realized that she might never see them again. In the past five years, she had gone from being the "little British refugee" to a fully Americanized young lady. Her life in Jersey, her mother, and the trip across the Atlantic seemed like a different life.

And then, just as the horn of the bus had sounded outside of the Grosvenor House Hotel five years earlier, the train's horn gave three short blasts, signaling that it was time for Jayne to board.

Little Jayne Jaffé was finally heading home.

\* \* \*

London had changed. Five years of war transformed the once-vibrant city into an environment of rubble and reconstruction. The war was finally over, but families still grieved the loss of loved ones. More than 300,000 British soldiers were alive when Jayne left, but now they were dead: lost at sea, buried in unmarked graves on distant battlefields or their corpses decaying where they had died in unknown places around the world.

American boys had suffered the same fates, but there was a huge difference between nations that had portions of a war fought on their own soil versus America, which, apart from Pearl Harbor, had remained free of enemy destruction.

Sailing east across the Atlantic, Jayne would not contemplate this difference. She didn't know what to expect when she arrived home, and unlike her sailing five years ago, there were no classes or briefings to prepare her or the other soon-to-be repatriated refugees for the next phase of their lives.

Jayne sailed from New York on the French liner SS *Ile de France*, the first major ocean liner built after the conclusion of World War I. Decorated entirely in the art deco style, it was considered one of the most beautifully appointed ships of the time. The dining hall towered three decks high and had a grand staircase for an entrance. The ship also had a neo-gothic-style chapel, a grand foyer that rose four decks, a shooting gallery, an elaborate gymnasium, and even a merry-go-round.

But now much of the ship's opulence was hidden, since the *Ile de France*, like most liners of the war era, had been converted into a troop transport. Many of the passengers were soldiers, assigned to Europe to help keep peace in liberated nations and help with reconstruction.

On board, Jayne was assigned a cabin number and a specific dining table. Meals were served at 7:30 a.m., noon, and 5:30 p.m., and lifeboat drills were held daily at 10:30 a.m. At night, entertainment included movies, performances by military bands, dances, and sing-a-longs.

Although shipboard life was predictable and routine, most of the refugees had limited knowledge of what they would face when they returned home. During the voyage they shared stories of their time in America, which were mostly happy recollections.

But others told about of the sufferings and hardships endured by their English families during the war. Some had lost their older brothers and fathers in battle or during the Blitzkrieg of 1940. Some would find their childhood home destroyed or gone or their mothers living with new husbands or dating a serious new boyfriend.

Then there were stories about some of the older British girls who had gotten themselves "heavy" (pregnant) while in America. They weren't on the *Ile de France* going home, nor would they ever be. They were outcasts, being told by their parents to never darken their doorstep again. Abortion was universally illegal and considered a criminal act, and pregnancy outside of marriage was equally forbidden.

Jayne's eventual reunion with her mother is best described by a letter Maureen sent to Helen Sullivan.

*83 Shirley Drive*
*Hove, England*

*25 September, 1945*

*My dear Helen,*

*It is a week ago today since Jayne arrived and with one thing and another, it's been a bit hectic!*

*I felt awfully nervous, waiting for her at the station, in case I didn't recognise her. But when the train came in we just knew each other at once, which was a great thrill. I didn't realize she was quite so tall – why, she has left me well behind. By our standards she looks about seventeen, but underneath, she's still quite a child, and a very nice one.*

*Before I continue with my first impressions which you asked me to write you, I want to thank you, Helen, for the way you've brought her up – and by that I don't mean the material things [you know what I feel about all that]. I mean her good manners, considerations for other people, and general outlook.*

*I'm afraid poor Jayne is going to miss you all very much – she thinks the world of you and, of course, hopes that we will be able to come over sometime, but heaven knows when that will be! Her heart is wholly American, and by America she means Milwaukee. My sister and various friends have extolled the virtues of California, but Jayne merely replied that they didn't know Milwaukee!*

*Poor child, I feel terribly sorry for her, because it's like starting all over again in a strange country and I only hope that we can get over [to America] some time.*

*I have fixed up for her to go to the convent of Our Lady of Zion and she starts next week. Unfortunately, the flat we were supposed to move into on Saturday won't be ready for another month – it has been badly blitzed* [bombed by the Germans] *and has to have quite extensive repairs, so she is going to be a weekly boarder until we move – quite the last thing I wanted after her being away so long.*

*I don't know whether Jayne told you in her letter that the trunk did not cross on the "Ile de France," but was sent over on the "Queen Mary" and is in England but hadn't yet been delivered.*

*Jayne has told us so much about you and the family that I almost feel I know you all and realize even more how wonderfully kind you have been. And thank you for all the lovely food – the oil and honey was a special treat. You've just been so kind that it isn't possible for me to thank you adequately.*

*Best wishes to you all.*

*Love,*
*Maureen*

For Jayne, the adjustment to life back in England was more challenging than her first weeks in America five years earlier. Nothing was as good, or as much fun, as it was with the Sullivans. Nor could it be. London had not only endured the Blitzkrieg, but it was the staging ground for nearly every Allied operation against Germany and for the liberation of Europe.

During the war, the island's population had swelled by nearly a half-million people. Soldiers, diplomats, war refugees, and newspaper and radio correspondents stressed the already short supplies of food, housing, clothing, and gasoline. It would take years, if not decades, for the United Kingdom to fully recover from the second Great War fought on its continent in the past 25 years.

Even the pastoral countryside was affected. American and British engineers felled forests, razed century-old cottages, and plowed up acres of farmland to build airbases for bomber and fighter aircraft. In Devon, along England's south coast, the British government evacuated 2,700 residents, without compensation, so that the Allies could stage a portion of the D-Day liberation of occupied France and, eventually, all of Europe.

Considering the magnitude of the D-Day plan, the need for vast amounts of housing and space became apparent. The invasion included more than 6,000 ships of all kinds (forming the largest armada in history), 326,000 troops, 12,000 aircraft, 54,000 vehicles including tanks, and 106,000 tons of supplies.

Most noticeable to Jayne, however, was the shortage of food. Rationing was still in effect, and meals consisted of products that were cheap, available, and filling such as potatoes, breads, and starchy concoctions of flour and cornmeal. Fresh vegetables, dairy products, and meats were difficult to find and required the use of many food rationing coupons.

This was a sharp contrast to America, where Jayne could buy most every type of food in the local grocery store without having to wait in line or present a rationing coupon. But here, Maureen had to save their coupons so they could afford a simple roast for the Sunday meal, the only meat Jayne ate during the week.

To help, the Sullivans and the Van Dykes sent food parcels and other items. Sweets were especially welcome, as the ration of lard was only two ounces per week, a tiny amount that could not be sacrificed for baking. Butter was available only in the finest restaurants and hotels and was virtually unattainable by regular citizens. At the request of Adj and Maureen, the Sullivans also shipped them cigarettes (nearly everybody in London smoked), stockings, sliced bacon, and chocolate.

Then there was the matter of school. Had Jayne remained in America, she would be entering her sophomore year at Downer Seminary. Maureen knew that Jayne's schooling in Milwaukee had been exceptional, so she decided to enroll her in one of London's best private schools, Our Lady of Zion, a Catholic girls' boarding school.

This was an expensive decision. Private boarding schools were affordable to only the wealthiest, yet somehow Maureen was able to afford the school's hefty tuition. More important, her decision to pay for Jayne's enrollment at a school attended by the sons and daughters of diplomats and ambassadors is testimony to her love for Jayne and her desire to give her the highest quality education possible.

In her first school year, Jayne took classes in French, Latin, English, biology, history, and geography. Mass was held every morning at 8:30, and regular prayer sessions occurred throughout the school day. Occasional "retreats" focused on religious studies when speaking was forbidden, and there was intensive instruction about the Catholic faith, God, and the saints.

Jayne hated Our Lady of Zion School. The nuns were humorless, strict, and not at all personable like the teachers at Downer Seminary or the Fox Point School. Everything was cold: cold food, cold water, cold buildings, and cold teachers. And there were no boys.

Jayne welcomed the weekends, when movies were the primary form of entertainment and also offered an escape from life in depressing London. Jayne saw *While the Sun Shines* and *Leave It to Heaven*, and pronounced them both "marvelous". She liked the movie *A Song to Remember* so much that she saw it six times.

In December 1945, her cousin Mary (Adj's daughter) got married, and Jayne was the bridesmaid. The reception included foods and beverages that most of the guests had not seen or consumed since the war had begun six years earlier. Particularly impressive was the serving of French champagne, an expensive luxury for the time.

Just a few weeks after Mary's wedding came Christmas Day, and Maureen was determined that the celebration be bountiful.

Throughout the year she had diligently saved money to give Jayne a holiday with ample gifts, food, and drink. And she succeeded. Jayne wrote to the Sullivans that for the first time since arriving home, "There was enough food to eat."

Jayne knew that her mother was bending over backward to make her life in England good and right and fun, so she was never critical of London life while in her presence. Even in her letters to the Sullivans, she seldom complained, preferring to write about her activities and how much she missed the Sullivans and life in Milwaukee. Jayne's tactful and sensitive demeanor, along with her maturity, continued to be evident in all she did.

Only one time did she tell how she truly felt, and that was in a letter to Bob and Bill Sullivan. Perhaps she felt that she could be less measured in her comments around her peers and American "brothers".

*Dear Bill and Bob,*

*I haven't had much time to write because right now I am boarding at school, only 'till our apartment has been repaired, thank goodness. A German bomb went through the building and made a mess of everything.*

*Boy, it really is horrible over here. First of all the way everyone talks drives me nuts. In the second place the food is horrible. You can't get anything decent and when you can get it you can't get enough.*

*I haven't been in a car since I've been here, which would kill both of you. I haven't seen a decent sized car. They are all the size of an Austin.*[15]

---

[15.] The Austin was a small automobile built between 1929 and 1934 by the American Austin Car Company in Butler, Pennsylvania. About 20,000 were produced.

*I hope you're enjoying yourself in school, I sure am not.*

*We had a lot of fun on the way over, and most of us were sorry to get home. We didn't do much on the boat except walk around all day, but at night there was always something going on.*

*I have to go to dinner now, but will try to finish later.*

*Just finished dinner. We had corned beef, lettuce, mashed potatoes and a poor imitation of chocolate pudding with custard over it.*

*In our class there is one French girl, a Spanish girl, an Italian girl and people from everywhere.*

*I have to go out now. Will write later.*

*Love,
Jayne*

Jayne was not alone in having to adapt to circumstances surrounding the reunion with her birth family. Her mother, like most every evacuee parent, had to adjust to a child who returned much different from when he or she left. Today, professional counseling would be made available to help both parents and children adapt, but in 1940s England, psychology was mostly unknown.

Most difficult for parents to accept was the Americanization of the child's language, dress, and demeanor. Britain has historically prided itself on its "civilized" ways, and many parents were horrified at their child's newly acquired mannerisms. The wearing of slacks, for example, a fashion trend among American women, was considered wholly unladylike and not becoming of British refinement.

There was also the matter of speech. All evacuees returned speaking "American", not British English. In many quarters, evacuee children were taunted with the shouts of "Yank, Yank, Yank!"

Worse, some evacuees were outright ostracized for having "fled" the war. Children who remained behind and had suffered through five years of food shortages, bombs, death, and destruction regarded the returning children as cowards and, in some cases, traitors to the Crown.

Maureen accepted the Americanized Jayne and so did most of Jayne's classmates at Our Lady of Zion School. But after spending one year as a boarding student, Jayne told Maureen that she preferred not to spend a second year living on campus, so Maureen made special arrangements for her to commute by public bus from their flat. It helped being able to go home at the end of each school day, but Jayne was still restless and dissatisfied. She decided not to return for her final, graduating year. Instead, she began looking for a job.

Work in postwar England was difficult to secure, but Jayne was determined. Almost any job seemed better than another year with the nuns, and perhaps she could earn money to help the household. She regularly browsed the "help wanted" ads in the *London Times*, rejecting most of the opportunities until she found one that advertised for an assistant to a commercial photographer. This job seemed different from the others.

Jayne immediately wrote a letter of introduction and addressed it to the box number listed in the ad. A week later, she received a reply from Colin Tait, owner of Colin Tait Commercial Photography: "Could you please make yourself available for an interview at my studio at Ten Bedford Square, London?"

Jayne went by herself and met Mr. Tait. An hour later, Jayne Jaffé, age 16, had her first job.

The work was not terribly difficult, and Jayne enjoyed it. She ran errands, typed letters, answered the telephone, and arranged photo sessions and dates with clients. Mr. Tait was an easygoing boss, the hours weren't long, and she had weekends free to spend time with her newfound love interest, Gerald Durrell. Gerald, two years older than Jayne, was intelligent, fun, and just handsome enough. For nine months they dated, going to movies and exploring the many sights of London.[16]

But Jayne's true love was elsewhere: 5,000 miles to the west, back in Fox Point and with the Sullivan family. Although she had been "home" for nearly three years, she still held strong affection for the country and family that had given her the best years of her life. She exchanged occasional letters with Bill and Helen, mostly sharing news of what she was doing, a little bit about her mother and Aunt Adj, and what life was like in postwar London. But those letters never told of her true desires and feelings.

One day she decided to change that. She penned a letter to Bill and Helen, telling them exactly what she wanted. She used stationary with a letterhead reading "COLIN TAIT, Photographer, Ten Bedford Square, London."

*September 17, 1947*

*Dear Uncle Bill,*

*I'm sorry I haven't written to you personally for such a long time but all the letters I write to Aunt Helen are meant for you too. I hear from the Krauses that you are all very well and that you are working much too hard.*

*I'll be quite honest and tell you that I have written for a particular reason. I have never been really happy since I got back and I don't feel that I will ever settle down properly. I've been wanting to get back to the States for a long time but I haven't done or said anything about it because my mother never seemed very enthusiastic. Now she says she will go over if she knows that there is a job for her. Otherwise she won't, which I can understand because it would be silly to spend*

---

[16.] Decades later, Jayne researched the whereabouts of Gerald Durrell and discovered that he founded a zoo in Jersey. Named the Durrell Zoo, it is still a popular attraction. Jayne wrote to him, but he never replied.

*all that money to get over and then find that there weren't any jobs. I would have to have one too, of course.*

*Please believe me when I say that I'm not trying to impose on you in any way because if you say that there aren't any jobs then I will at least have the satisfaction of having tried. I'm asking you all this because I'm sure you know what the position is. I'm very anxious to get back if I possibly can. I've even thought of stowing away on a ship but I thought that wasn't a very good idea after a while.*

*Also there's the question of finding somewhere to live which I suppose isn't so easy. I have to ask you to find out about all this but if you could just ask a couple people I would be very grateful. I owe you such a lot already that I'm sure this little thing wouldn't make much difference. I hope some day I can repay a little of it in some way or other. You'll never know how happy I am that I was with you for those five years. I didn't realise what you were doing for me then but I am just beginning to know now.*

*After reading this over it sounds rather like an epistle but I'm going to leave it because I mean every word of it.*

*Give my love to Aunt Helen and the boys (I guess I shouldn't call them that any more) and I hope very much to see you all within the next year.*

*Love,*
*Jayne*

Writing the letter was a courageous step. Not only was Jayne inquiring about a return visit, but she was asking Bill to find jobs and housing that could lead to her, and perhaps her mother's, permanent resettlement in the United States. Via that letter, it was now Jayne, not Maureen, who was making plans for their future.

On September 22, 1947, Bill Sullivan dictated a reply to his secretary and had the letter addressed to Jayne at 12A Clarendon Court, London W9, England.

*Dear Jayne:*

*I was delighted to receive your letter of September 17th, and of course will do everything I can to help you and your mother to come to this country. From everything I hear of conditions in England I feel quite sure that your decision is the only sensible one to make.*

*I am certain we will be able to find jobs for both of you, since there is a shortage of help in almost all classifications in this country. Housing, of course, is a more serious problem, but I feel equally confident we will be able to find something for you. However, there is no point in looking for a place until we know approximately when you will arrive. I suggest that you inquire at the American Consulate as to how long it will take you to get the necessary visas and when you will probably arrive in this country, and I can then go to work with a definite date in mind.*

*Under our laws you will be required to go to school one day a week until you are 18 years of age; your birth record is necessary to verify your age.*

*I am writing to John Friend and asking him to call on you and your mother to discuss this matter the next time he is in London. I am sure if you have any quota difficulties that he will be very helpful.*

*Both of the boys left for school a week ago and from their letter and one telephone conversation are enjoying themselves tremendously.*

> When you write again I would appreciate your letting me know in detail the type of work your mother has been doing and what her preferences are. I have already mentioned your letter to Mr. Madden, and he said that if you were interested he would be glad to have you in his office as an assistant cashier or in some similar position. I shall make further inquiries and let you know developments from time to time.
>
> Love,
> Uncle Bill

Uncle Bill's letter left out an important truth: things had changed in the Sullivan home. The idyllic, happy family of Fox Point that Jayne remembered had become cold and emotionally empty. Bill Jr. and Bob were away at boarding school, and his marriage to Helen was disintegrating. And as much as he missed Jayne, he did not want her to witness the unhappy state of his family life. Jayne would be "coming home" to a much separated family, and Bill and Helen worried about how Jayne would react. They vowed to present a happy front, at least in her presence.

Maureen shared Jayne's unhappiness in London, but for different reasons. As a mother, she had the instinctive desire to ensure her child's well-being, but she could only do so much. She couldn't eliminate the challenges of living in postwar England, nor could she magically improve her financial position or living arrangements.

Further, Jayne was no longer the little girl who clutched her hand while boarding the ship from Jersey to London in 1940. Jayne was a young woman, independent and capable of living on her own. Maureen had unfailingly tried to make Jayne "an English person" once again, but after three years, Maureen acknowledged that Jayne's ties were no longer to England but to America.

Maureen hoped that Jayne would want to go home to Jersey, but it was clear that Jayne had moved beyond that part of her life. Maureen contemplated going back alone, but the thought of leaving her only child, especially after five years of separation, was unthinkable. But staying in London wasn't an option, either.

Uncle Bill's promise of finding housing and work helped Maureen acquiesce to Jayne's desire to return to America. If it didn't work out, Maureen thought, she could return to London or Jersey, knowing she had been with Jayne until full adulthood.

So on October 13, 1947, she penned a letter to Bill Sullivan.

*Dear Mr. Sullivan,*

*First of all I want to thank you for offering to help us get settled in Milwaukee. As you know, no other part of the U.S. counts to Jayne, and she's been pining to get back ever since she left, and I realize now that she will never feel really at home over here.*

*We went to the American Consulate last week and got the necessary forms. Amazingly enough there seem to be no quota difficulties for British people, but it is necessary to have sponsors and guaranteed employment.*

*Now, I don't know what type of job I would be suitable for in the U.S. I am labor manager and welfare officer of a small chemical factory, but I realize I couldn't do an equivalent job with you, as I do not know your industrial law and trade union agreements.*

*Anyhow, I'm adaptable and open to any suggestions you have – the main things are a reasonable wage and living accommodations.*

*I won't attempt to really thank you for all your kindness until we meet. In the meantime, my best wishes to you and my love to Helen.*

*Yours sincerely,*
*Maureen Jaffé*

Jayne followed with her own letter.

*Dear Aunt Helen,*

*I just want to say how much we appreciate everything you both are doing for us. I'm looking forward to this trip so much. We have booked our train passage from New York to Milwaukee through American Express. I don't think we will be in New York more than a few days. As far as I'm concerned I'd just as soon go straight through.*

*I'm not going to say any more now except that I'm longing to see you and Uncle Bill more than I can say. I hope you won't be too shocked when you see me.*

*Love,*
*Jayne*

## - VII -

## *The American Dream*

In the spring of 1948, nearly three years after Jayne had returned from Milwaukee, Maureen bought two tickets of passage to New York City on the *Queen Mary*, the magnificent flagship of the Cunard Line. They bid farewell to Adj, and on April 15 boarded the finest ocean liner in the world at Southampton.

Onboard, Maureen and Jayne immediately set out to explore the ship's parlors, dining rooms, promenades, game rooms, pool, and gymnasiums. But they discovered that the grandeur was gone. During the war, the *Queen Mary* had been converted into a troop ship for ferrying Allied soldiers. During that transition, the Cunard Line removed six miles of fine carpet and 220 cases of china, crystal, and silver, and covered the ornate wood walls with leather. The stateroom furniture and decor was removed, and 6,000 bunk beds were added. Throughout the war, up to 15,000 men at a time would sail to and from Europe on a liner built to accommodate just over 2,000 passengers.

Since the liner was also painted gray to camouflage her from the enemy, she was now referred to as the "Gray Ghost". But she was still an oceangoing marvel, capable of steaming along at a record-setting 32 knots, making her faster than the German U-boats and able to finish the Atlantic crossing in less than a week.

Uncle Bill arranged for Maureen and Jayne to be met in New York by his good friend Clifford Morehouse. Not only would it be good for Maureen and Jayne to have a few days in New York to recover from the voyage, it would give Jayne a chance to see Bill and Bob, who were attending a private boarding school in nearby Connecticut.

In a letter dated March 26, 1948, Uncle Bill wrote to his friend Clifford Morehouse:

> *Dear Cliff:*
>
> *Mrs. Jaffé has written that she and Jayne are going to spend several days visiting with you on their way to Milwaukee, and if it is not too great an inconvenience, I would appreciate it if arrangements could be made for them to see Bill and Bob who are at the Choate School at Wallingford, Connecticut. I am under the impression that this is only a short distance from your home, and if someone could drive them over, I know the boys would be very pleased.*

Then, in a separate letter to Maureen, he wrote, in part,

> *I presume this will be the last opportunity to write you before you leave, and I want you to know that both Mrs. Sullivan and I are looking forward with a great deal of anticipation to your arrival, and, of course, we are particularly anxious to see Jayne again.*

Jayne was anxious to see the Sullivans again as well. On the trans-Atlantic crossing she told her mother all about Milwaukee, the Sullivans, and her school chums. Returning to America was the culmination of years of anticipation, and now it was happening.

For her part, Maureen was gratified that Jayne was happy. But America was not familiar to Maureen, and she felt as if she was trading one set of stresses for another. Postwar London was dismal, for sure, but at least it was familiar. Now she was heading to the land of ample and luxurious living, but everything was going to be different. It was Jayne's world, not hers.

Uncle Bill and Aunt Helen were waiting for them at Milwaukee's Chicago & Northwestern depot, the towering edifice of Romanesque red brick with a 234-foot clock tower. Waving and smiling as they approached each other, the Sullivans and Jaffés embraced. Through his tears, Uncle Bill told them how happy he was to see them, marveling how much Jayne had grown, and saying what an honor it was to meet Maureen after all these years.

As they walked through the cavernous main hall of the depot, Jayne talked incessantly. She had waited years for this moment, and all of her thoughts and emotions were spilling out at once. She asked about her friends and the Sullivans' house, and she listed all the places she wanted her mother to see.

And how magnificent everything looked! It was springtime in Milwaukee, the grass was lush, there were fat buds on the trees, and the sun was warm on her face. Like nature emerging after a dark winter, Jayne too felt that her life was renewed.

The Sullivans asked about the voyage on the *Queen Mary*, and Jayne replied that it was "fine" and continued her excited monologue. Maureen was quiet, overwhelmed by meeting the Sullivans and finally seeing the city that was the focus of her daughter's life.

They boarded the Sullivans' luxurious four-door sedan for the ride home. It was larger than any vehicle Maureen had ever seen except for cars in the movies. As they left the depot, she watched the scenery from the back seat. Most noticeable was Lake Michigan. Jayne had told her about Milwaukee's "big lake", but to Maureen, a lake was a body of water where you could see the opposite shore. This lake resembled an ocean.

Uncle Bill rolled down the window to let in the fresh spring air. Jayne said, "Mummy, there are many beautiful homes up ahead; they'll remind you of the English countryside!"

Other than Lake Michigan, which looked like the English Channel, Maureen hadn't seen much that reminded her of home. Everything was so spread out, so impersonal. Where were the street-side cafes with people sipping coffee beside outdoor tables? And where were the flower gardens, the fountains, and the vendors selling goods from their carts?

They drove up a small hill, leaving the lake behind. For the next few miles, they passed the stately homes reminiscent of those owned by British dukes and duchesses, the highest ranked people of nonroyal blood in England. Maureen wondered if the Sullivans' home would be as elegant. And if it was, how should she react? She didn't want the Sullivans to think of her as a "poor little London girl", but the reality was that Maureen had spent nearly a decade living in a tiny flat in a city rife with wartime destruction.

After a few more miles, Uncle Bill slowed the car and announced their arrival. Maureen was relieved; the house wasn't as opulent as those she had seen earlier, but still, it was a world apart from anything she had ever lived in. Jayne opened the car door and tugged at her mother's arm. "Come on, Mummy, let me show you the house!" Uncle Bill tended to the luggage while Jayne, Maureen, and Aunt Helen went inside.

For the first time, Jayne was silent. Leaving her mother and Aunt Helen in the entry hall, she went to explore the many rooms to see if anything had changed. To her pleasure, everything appeared the same, from the grandfather clock in the living room to the big black telephone on the little wooden stand in the kitchen. Even Bill and Bob's bedroom had their favorite baseball bats standing in the corner and the jar full of pennies on the dresser, even though both boys were now at school in Connecticut.

Jayne toured her mother through the home, saving her bedroom for the very end. As they entered, Jayne became misty-eyed at the sight of her mother in the place she has slept for so many nights. There was the small bed where she had read her mother's letters, dreamed about her at night, and at times missed her terribly. Now her mother was with her, in the very room where she had spent years wondering if she'd ever see her again.

Maureen put her arms around Jayne and hugged her. It was the most intimate moment they had shared since Jayne boarded the big ship for America eight years earlier. As they embraced, Maureen saw a photo of herself that remained on Jayne's dresser. Maybe now, in America, they could finally rekindle their long-lost mother-daughter relationship.

*This Token of Freedom*

That night, Aunt Helen cooked a "welcome home" dinner. Seated around the table in the large dining room beneath a crystal chandelier, Maureen marveled at the array of foods, many of which she hadn't seen since the war began. There were ample portions of sliced beef tenderloin, freshly steamed asparagus, buttery mashed potatoes, gravies, and a salad with tomatoes, onions, slivered carrots, and a rich dressing called Thousand Island. To have a meal like this in London would have required Maureen to save money and rationing coupons for at least a month. Here, it seemed like the Sullivans could eat this way every night.

Uncle Bill opened his finest bottle of red wine, and then another. Maureen drank two or three glasses, savoring the rich vineyard flavors she hadn't known since her days of hosting parties with her husband Jack on Jersey Island. Warmed by the wine, Maureen felt dreamy and content. She was in a big American home, with seemingly endless amounts of food, and her daughter was sitting next to her. Whatever concerns she had about leaving London had, at least for now, vanished.

That night, in a queen-size bed in her room with its own private bath, Maureen slept soundly for 14 hours.

\* \* \*

After a few days of acclimation at the Sullivan home, Uncle Bill offered good news. He had found work for both Maureen and Jayne. That was the easy part. Finding housing was more difficult, but he was successful in securing an apartment for them in the Ardmore, a building located at 16th Street and Wisconsin Avenue, in the vicinity of present-day Marquette University. "It's pretty basic," warned Uncle Bill, "but housing is hard to find and it's clean, safe, and in a convenient location." And Uncle Bill had already paid their first month's rent.

Then he discussed the jobs. "They're good jobs," he promised, with decent pay and at reliable companies. Maureen would work in personnel for the George J. Meyer Bottling Company, the world's largest producer of automatic bottling and bottle-cleaning equipment. The Meyer family were acquaintances of the Sullivans, and they resided in a luxurious home in Whitefish Bay, a village neighboring Fox Point.[17]

Jayne would work as a secretary for Lou Madden, the father of her school chum, Ann, at the downtown Milwaukee office of his insurance company, Kansas City Life.

Considering that the average yearly salary in 1948 was about $3,400, Maureen likely earned about $2,400 for her work, and Jayne earned considerably less. Consumer costs, still inflated after the war, caused gasoline to spike up to 26 cents per gallon (just 10 years earlier it was about 5 cents per gallon), a loaf of bread was 14 cents, and it cost 3 cents to send a letter. The sticker price of a new car was $1,500, which made them unaffordable for most. Nearly 40 percent of American homes still lacked indoor plumbing.

Their Ardmore apartment lived up to Uncle Bill's description. It was "pretty basic," with two bedrooms, a small kitchen and living area, and windows overlooking Wisconsin Avenue. Just below the windows was the top of the overhang that sheltered the front entrance. There were a few small grocery stores and a couple of taverns within walking distance, but the area seemed impersonal to Maureen, and not at all like the chummy districts of London, which felt like little towns within a big city.

Still, the neighborhood was safe, and the public bus stopped less than a block from their door, where both Jayne and Maureen boarded it for work and then rode it back home again. The bus ran along Wisconsin Avenue, Milwaukee's main thoroughfare, making it convenient for Maureen to stop and buy groceries or other household necessities.

Although the people of Milwaukee were friendly, Maureen encountered nobody who shared her British heritage. How nice

---

17. For 50 years, between 1935 and 1985, the Meyers had an annual tradition of celebrating the 4th of July with a spectacular fireworks display. Their event attracted hundreds onto the hillside in adjacent Klode Park along the shore of Lake Michigan. The celebration served as the village's fireworks during those years.

*This Token of Freedom*

it would have been, she thought, to speak with somebody who appreciated and understood her life back in the Motherland.

Instead, Maureen noticed that Milwaukee was replete with Poles and Germans. Both groups had made a strong cultural imprint on the city. Milwaukee boasted several fine German restaurants – some of the best outside of Germany, many claimed. There were also large brewing companies with German names like Schlitz, Pabst, and Miller. The breweries were among the town's largest employers, and Maureen noticed that beer seemed to be a Milwaukeean's beverage of choice.

Mitchell Street, just to the south, was the heart of a large Polish district, and was once Milwaukee's main shopping district before everything moved north to the Wisconsin Avenue region. One afternoon, out of curiosity, Maureen and Jayne spent an afternoon on Mitchell Street and heard more Polish spoken than English.

Maureen liked the Polish people and even sympathized with them since their country had suffered greatly during the war. Unlike England, which remained free of Nazi occupation, Poland was brutally invaded in 1939 and ruled with an oppressive Nazi hand. Millions of Jews were separated from their families and deported to concentration camps, built on Polish soil, where their lives were slowly ended. Maureen would be forever grateful to the skilled Polish pilots who had helped the Royal Air Force stave off German occupation of England during the Battle of Britain.

Because of her recent memories of Nazi destruction and inhumanity, Maureen tried to avoid everything that was German in Milwaukee, a difficult task given the city's cultural heritage. Each time she heard a person speaking German, she wondered if they had a relative who was part of the Nazi war machine, the evil people whose imperialistic ambitions had forced her and Jayne to leave Jersey. How much better everyone's lives would have been if Hitler and the Nazis were never voted into power.

Maureen also felt underemployed and unappreciated at the bottling company, and within a year she had grown weary of Milwaukee and her job. She needed a change but wasn't quite ready to leave Jayne and return to England.

Since arriving in the United States, Maureen had harbored thoughts about seeing California, specifically Hollywood. A friend who lived there had extended an invitation to visit, but Maureen decided she wanted to do more than see Hollywood as a tourist. She wanted to live there and experience it all up close.

At the time, Hollywood was in the midst of its "golden era", and the 1940s produced many of the industry's most creative and stellar films. As actor David Niven wrote in his autobiography *Bring on the Empty Horses*:

> Hollywood bore very little relationship to the rest of the world, but it was vastly exciting to be a part of the greatest form of mass entertainment so far invented. Over 200,000,000 people each week would pay to see movies, and among the names in lights above their theaters were Garbo, Gable, Astaire, Cooper, Grant, Chaplin, Bogart, Garland, Hepburn, Flynn and Davis. It was a fascinating canvas, and there will never be another like it.

There were several reasons for Hollywood's popularity. In the pre-television era, movies were the primary form of visual entertainment, and movie theaters were considered a necessity in every town, regardless of size. If a town didn't have a movie theater, it was considered backward and boring. In large cities, movie theaters were often built to opulent standards, akin to the finest hotels of the era. In Detroit, for example, movie theater magnate John Kunsky built more than 20 theaters that seated up to 3,300 people each.

But most important to the times (and very different from today), Hollywood was viewed as a patriotic and helpful war ally. Every feature film was preceded by a 10-minute newsreel that documented the latest war battles and progress. During the war, wildly popular actors and actresses such as Rita Hayworth volunteered their time to promote war bonds, military enlistment, scrap metal drives, and rationing and offered household tips for helping our "boys fighting overseas". Several of the major stars served in combat, including Jimmy Stewart, bomber pilot, and Clark Gable, bomber crew gunner.

In early 1949, Maureen asked Jayne if she'd like to resettle with her to Hollywood. The thought of another move seemed inconvenient to Jayne; she felt as if the past four years were little more than a series of life transitions, and now her mother was proposing another one. Jayne had a good job and many friends, and she was comfortably settled with her mother.

But Hollywood was the golden city, the place of movie stars, palm trees, sunshine, and beautiful people. Of all the places to relocate, it seemed the most appealing. Perhaps Maureen would find a husband. Maybe Jayne would find a boyfriend. Maybe it was the place where everyone would live happily ever after, just like in the movies.

Jayne resigned her job with Lou Madden and Kansas City Life, and Maureen happily quit her situation at the Meyer Bottling Company. Then they told the Sullivans about their plans.

Bill and Helen were enthused about the move, probably because their marital situation continued to deteriorate. It would be less embarrassing to endure divorce proceedings if Jayne and Maureen were away. Uncle Bill even offered to contact a friend who owned a marine insurance company, Johnson & Higgins, in Hollywood. Perhaps he could use an employee like Jayne. Heck Powell, the uncle of Jayne's good friend Nancy Powell, lived in Pasadena with his wife, and they offered to help Maureen and Jayne get settled. So in February 1949, Maureen and Jayne boarded the train in Milwaukee for the three-day ride to Los Angeles to discover the world of Hollywood and fashionable southern California.

Once again, Jayne was traveling to an environment completely foreign from what she had left. While most British adults had lived their entire lives in one place, Jayne had already moved from Jersey to London to Boston to Milwaukee, then back to London and again to Milwaukee. Now she was heading to the glamour of Hollywood and southern California. For an 18-year-old girl in 1949, she had led a very worldly life.

Unlike Milwaukee, which seemed to shut down during the winter, Hollywood was always bustling. The sun shone year-round, and there were many sights to see. Maureen and Jayne lived like tourists, visiting Knott's Berry Farm, Grauman's Chinese Theater, and the beach, looking for movie stars in Beverly Hills and strolling the Santa Monica pier and boardwalk.

Since the latest films usually premiered in the local theaters, Maureen and Jayne saw them before the rest of the country. Some of Hollywood's finest motion pictures were released in 1949, including *The Third Man*, starring Orson Wells and Joseph Cotton. Filmed on location in postwar Vienna, it offered an architecturally compelling view of the war-ravaged city and revealed an atmosphere of mistrust, lawlessness, and fear during a time of socio-economic rebuilding.

The war provided thrilling themes for other box-office hits, including *Twelve O'clock High*, a film about American air crews in the Army's Eighth Air Force who flew daylight bombing missions against Germany. *The Sands of Iwo Jima*, starring John Wayne, documented a group of United States Marines from their initial training to their participation in the Battle of Iwo Jima, one of the bloodiest battles of the war, in which the Marines took 25,000 casualties (killed or wounded). All three movies won Academy Awards in 1949.

The public craved these stories of heroism, and pride in the United States was strong. Maureen found the movies entertaining but told Jayne that they portrayed a biased and overly dramatic view of Americans in combat. Many films left the impression that America alone had defeated the Nazis and Japan. Maureen knew otherwise; Britain was fighting the war long before America entered the conflict, and her soldiers had already fought many heroic battles. But for now, there was no significant movie industry in England to tell their stories.

Hunting for movie stars was a popular pastime for locals and tourist alike. Before television, actors and actresses enjoyed huge popular attention. Fan magazines, newspaper columns, and radio broadcasts followed every detail of a star's life. Fans stalked the popular screen idol hangouts like the Brown Derby Restaurant and other fashionable clubs and restaurants of Beverly Hills.

When they had saved enough money, Jayne and Maureen indulged in a visit to the Ambassador Hotel's Coconut Grove

Nightclub in downtown Los Angeles. There they saw Ava Gardner and Frank Sinatra and hoped to see other famous Hollywood luminaries such as Glenn Ford, Bette Davis, or Elizabeth Taylor.

In 1949, live music was common in most upscale restaurants and nightclubs. The "big band" style, which began in the 1920s, remained popular, and Benny Goodman, Gene Krupa, and Glenn Miller were household names. The song "Ghost Riders in the Sky," sung by the handsome and tuxedo-clad Vaughn Monroe in his deep soothing voice, topped the charts. The lyrics told about an old cowboy chasing a mythical herd of red-eyed cows "a-plowin' through the ragged skies". (In 1979, Johnny Cash recorded his own version, and the song's popularity was resurrected 30 years later.)

Hollywood was a world unto itself, removed from the realities of life in most American towns and certainly in Europe. Overseas, London continued to recover from wartime, and the German capital of Berlin, once the most beautiful city in all of Europe, was now a wasteland of destruction whose citizens remained on the verge of starvation.

Meanwhile, the Soviet Union, an ally of the United States during WWII, had become the latest threat to American freedom. Since the war's conclusion, the Soviets had installed Communist dictatorship in Poland, Hungary, the Baltic states of Lithuania, Estonia, and Latvia, and most recently by coup in Czechoslovakia. Now they threatened to control Berlin by blockading food and fuel deliveries to the sectors controlled by England, France, and the United States.[18]

Closer to home, rumors abounded that the United States would be Russia's next military target. In 1949, America's armed forces were in serious postwar decline, while Russia was engaged in massive

---

[18.] The Soviet blockade of the western sectors of Berlin was an attempt to force England, France, and the United States to withdraw from Berlin, effectively conceding the "free" sectors of Berlin to the Communists. This action prompted the historic Berlin Airlift, in which the American military flew thousands of tons of supplies into Berlin's Tempelhof Airport. Not only did the airlift defeat the Soviet blockade, but it created immense German goodwill toward the Americans, their former wartime adversary.

military expansion. The only way America could defeat Russia in a military conflict would be through the use of a nuclear weapon. The cold war with the Soviet Union had begun, and many Americans lived in fear of a Russian attack and possible nuclear destruction.

Although the comforts of beautiful Hollywood kept Maureen from contemplating another war, they couldn't keep her from longing for home, even though life in post-war England remained difficult. Unlike Jayne, who had become fully Americanized, Maureen was still British, feeling disoriented in a country that shared almost nothing of the customs and traditions of England. Maureen retained a British accent and still used British vernacular for many common items. She missed the politeness and civility of British life. To her, Americans were loud, often uncouth, and too materialistic and competitive. In every respect, she was still a "Jersey girl" who felt misplaced in big, impersonal America.

Jayne felt sad about her mother's discomfort. She had hoped her mother would love America as she did, but it was not to happen. Instead, she knew her mother had suffered silently through her time in America. After all, when the war ended, she had always wanted to go home to Jersey.

But like so many parents of her generation, Maureen did not live for herself, so she dedicated her life to what she thought was best for her daughter. She went to America. And despite feeling lonely and often out of place, she kept the British "stiff upper lip" and abided by the signs in the London bomb shelters: "keep calm and carry on."

So the inevitable conversation happened: Maureen told Jayne she was going home to Jersey. She missed her friends, her former home, the Pooleys, and the business of J.H. Jaffé & Company. She also knew that Jayne was a mature and independent woman, capable of finding her own way in the world.

"It always seemed that way", Maureen thought. Even when Jayne left for America on August 10, 1940, she seemed capable of being on her own. In reflection, Maureen knew that after that day of separation, their relationship had ceased to be one of mother-daughter. During the most formative years of Jayne's life,

Maureen never held her hand, cried with her, took her to shows, attended her school functions, or participated in any of the activities of traditional parents.

Maureen and Jayne were adult women and close friends. They loved each other and carried a mutual respect for what each of them had endured during their separation, but the consequences of war had kept them from bonding in a traditional mother-daughter fashion during the most impressionable years of their lives.

Those were years they would never get back. But at least they had survived them. Many hadn't. The obituaries in the London papers carried daily notices of mothers and fathers lost to war and bombs. In America and other evacuee nations, many children were influenced so negatively that they would be tormented for the rest their lives.

But now, in late autumn of 1949, at the Los Angeles airport, Maureen was alive and well, and Jayne was a well-adjusted young lady. They hugged for a long time, knowing it might be years before they saw each other again. In a way, it was like parting as they did in London nine years earlier. But this time there was no threat of war; Maureen was going home to Jersey, and Jayne was happily living in America. Everything had turned out all right after all, and Maureen was thankful.

Yes, the times had changed. Maureen's return trip home would be by air, not by sea or rail. With rapid advances in aviation, long-distance flying was becoming a reality. In the late 1940s, airline passengers could fly from Los Angeles to New York, with one stop, in just over 12 hours.

Maureen's flight was called for boarding, and she walked onto the tarmac, turned around, and waved one last time to Jayne. Then she claimed her seat on the most sophisticated passenger aircraft in the air, the Lockheed Constellation – a huge, four-engine, propeller-driven aircraft, sleek and modern. The entire 6,000-mile trip from Los Angeles to London would take an astoundingly fast three days.

On both flights, Maureen would be occupied by her thoughts and a book, as in-flight movies or music did not exist. Since there were no fold-down tables, meals were served by placing a tray of food on the passenger's lap. While Maureen reclined in her seat at 24,000 feet above the ocean, she wondered how many lives would have been saved if evacuees could have escaped Britain by plane instead of spending weeks afloat on the hostile north Atlantic.

Meanwhile, Jayne returned to the West Hollywood apartment. Without her mother, it seemed sterile and foreign. She continued to work for a few more weeks while longing for Milwaukee, the Sullivans, and her friends. Wisconsin had been home for many years, her umbilical cord to Jersey and England long ago severed.

Weeks later she resigned her job with Johnson & Higgins Insurance Company and booked a train ticket to Milwaukee. Then she wrote to Uncle Bill and Aunt Helen.

The first lines of her letter were what she'd wanted to write for years. Now she could. When she put pen on paper and watched the ink flow into shapes of letters, she felt so natural, so happy, so wonderful. They were the culmination of everything she had known and felt since she left for London at the war's conclusion. They were the most beautiful words she'd ever written.

*Dear Uncle Bill and Aunt Helen,*

*I'm coming home.*

# AFTERWORD

As the handbook promised, Jayne Jaffé went on to live the promise of America's token of freedom. She married at age 19, had two children, Lynne and Michael, and enjoyed a successful career as an investment advisor. She lives in Whitefish Bay, Wisconsin, a suburb of Milwaukee, and now has eight grandchildren.

After Maureen left Hollywood and returned to Jersey in 1949, she was content for the first time in 10 years. The war was over, and she was home. The air smelled as fresh as ever, a combination of salt water, soil, and leaves that was unique to the island. She found a comfortable flat in St. Helier (the Jaffé home was likely wrecked beyond repair), socialized with her friends, and occasionally helped the Pooleys run J.H. Jaffé & Company, which had maintained its financial solvency during the German occupation.

She made one return visit to the United States to see Jayne and meet her new granddaughter, Lynne, in 1955. Shortly after she returned home, Maureen lunched with friends in St. Helier. Thereafter, back at her flat, she told her housekeeper that she was feeling ill. She went to bed and never awakened. Maureen Jaffé was 54 years old. Her lunch friends said she was wonderfully happy and relaxed during her final meal. She is buried next to her husband in a small Jersey cemetery.

The Sullivan home on East Thorne Lane, in Fox Point still exists. The home was built for Willis Sullivan and his family in the 1930s, and they were the original owners and occupants.

J.H. Jaffé & Company was liquidated in early 2011, but its retail subsidiary, Jersey Paint and Wallpaper Company, remains in business, and Jayne remains a shareholder.

Bill Sullivan passed away in 1987 and Helen Sullivan in 1995.

Bill Sullivan Jr. passed away in 2005, and his brother Bob Sullivan passed away in 2006.

After the war, the SS *Samaria,* the liner on which Jayne sailed from Liverpool to New York in 1940, was refitted to carry only 900 passengers and returned to life as a pleasure cruise ship. In January 1956, she was scrapped at Inverkeithing, Scotland.

The SS *Ile de France*, the ship that returned Jayne to England at the conclusion of World War II, was scrapped in Japan in 1952.

The *Queen Mary*, the liner on which Jayne and her mother sailed to America in 1948, was retired from service in 1972 and is now a hotel and tourist attraction moored in Long Beach, California.

At the time of this publication, Aunt Adj's daughter, Mary, is 93 years old and living in the Cotswold's in England.

Jayne is still good friends with most of the girls she met while living with the Sullivans in Fox Point.

Irene Hildebrand, Jayne's fifth-grade teacher at the Fox Point Elementary School and the woman who became her "school mom", kept in touch with Jayne throughout her life and even visited her when she returned to London after the conclusion of the war.

Jayne has made several trips back to Jersey. In 1970, she took her children Lynne and Michael with her and introduced them to both Jersey and London.

## THE END

# ABOUT THE AUTHOR

Jon Helminiak is an author, pilot, scuba diver, wilderness kayaker/canoeist, historian and global adventurer. He has pioneered many remote regions via solo kayak expeditions including the coast of Arabia and the islands west of Papua New Guinea.

Helminiak has held leadership positions at the University of Wisconsin-Milwaukee, the University of Wisconsin Foundation, and the Manito-wish YMCA. He is president of Adventure Quest Productions, co-founder of Pax Media Corporation, and a consultant to non-profit organizations.

*This Token of Freedom* is his fifth published book.

His Website is Adventurequestproductions.com

# ALSO BY JON HELMINIAK

*Nothing Routine* – A Quest for Adventure in Remote and Strange Places

*Land O' Lakes* – The History

*Course Set for Manito-wish* – The History

*Influence!* The Wisdom of Elmer F. Ott

CPSIA information can be obtained at www.ICGtesting.com
Printed in the USA
LVOW081338120513

333380LV00001B/4/P